On the Legitimate Interpretation of Holy Scripture

As attested by the judgments of the outstanding theologians
Dr. Polycarp Leyser and Balthasar Mentzer

and

Written by the work and effort of
Johann Gerhard,
Doctor of Sacred Theology
And Superintendent of Heldburg.

Rom. 12:6: "Having [the gift of] prophecy, let him prophesy according to the measure of his faith."

Attended by the grace and privilege
of the Electors and Dukes of Saxony

Published at Jena
in the shop and at the cost of Tobias Steinmann
In the year 1610

Translated by the Rev. Dr. Richard J. Dinda, Prof. Em.

✦REPRISTINATION PRESS✦
MALONE, TEXAS

A translation of Johann Gerhard, *Tractatus de legitima Scripturæ Sacræ Interpretatione* (1610). Copyright 2015 by Richard Dinda. Published by permission of the translator. No part of this publication may be reproduced, stored in a retrieval system, or transmitted in any form or by any means, electronic, mechanical, photocopying or otherwise without the prior written permission of Repristination Press.

Published in 2015.

REPRISTINATION PRESS
P.O. BOX 173
BYNUM, TEXAS 76631

www.repristinationpress.com

ISBN 1-891469-68-1

Foreword.

Over two decades have now passed since Repristination Press published its first new translation from the works of Johann Gerhard. Although this endeavor was belittled by some at the time, the flourishing efforts to publish translations from several of the confessional Lutheran fathers demonstrate that, by the grace of the Triune God, our labors have not been in vain. Where once there were those who claimed that some of Gerhard's most important works were essentially impossible to publish in an English translation, the burgeoning list of such published works bespeaks the shortsightedness of those who have imagined the Church should be fed with lesser fare. Now that one of the most significant works produced by the Lutheran fathers—the *Harmony of the Evangelists* written by Martin Chemnitz, Polycarp Leyser and Johann Gerhard—is appearing in an English edition, one may hope that the renewed interest in the confessional Lutheran fathers is far from spent.

It is a great joy to publish Dr. Richard Dinda's translation of Johann Gerhard's *Tractatus de legitima Scripturæ Sacræ Interpretatione* (1610). Dr. Dinda's efforts to offer the English-speaking world the writings of Johann Gerhard and Nicolaus Hunnius have been, and continue to be, a blessing to the Church.

+*James D. Heiser, M.Div., S.T.M.*
Bishop, the Evangelical Lutheran Diocese of North America
Publisher, Repristination Press

[Dedicatory Letter]

[p. i]¹ To the energetic and eminent Lord Valentinus à Selwitz, a very noble man of long-standing splendor of family and erudition and renowned for his deeds, a Franconian knight, an hereditary [*hæreditario*] in Eindo and Sempershausen, chief counsel of the provincial court of Coberg, counsel for the courts of Saxony and Brandenburg, as well as governor, lord, and his own Maecenas in Cadelsburg:

Hearty greetings and a happy beginning of this year!

Energetic and eminent sir, a Maecenas worthy of our respect: That is an outstanding statement of Bishop Irenaeus of Lyons, a very old writer of the Church, with which he begins the first chapter of Bk. 3 of his *Against Heresies:* "We have not learned of the arrangement of our salvation through others as much as we have through them (the apostles), through whom the Gospel has reached us. They indeed proclaimed the Gospel at that time. [p.ii] Later, however, through the will of God they handed down what would be the foundation and structure of our faith."

In this statement, Irenaeus presents to us four chief points which are very worthy of our mention. The first is that we have come to a knowledge of our salvation through the apostles. The author himself explains this in the preface of the aforementioned Bk. 3; namely, that the Lord of all gave His apostles the power of the Gospel. Through them, we have also come to know the teaching of the Son of God. In Irenaeus, therefore, we have a close connection among the power

---

1 The pagination of the 1610 edition shall thus be noted throughout this translation.

of the Gospel, heavenly truth, the teaching of Christ, the preaching of the apostles, and the arrangement of our salvation.

Second, the apostles reduced that very Gospel which they had proclaimed into writing. Third, that happened through the will of God. Fourth, those writings of the apostles or, what is the same, the Gospel which the apostles reduced to writing, are the foundation and structure of our faith.

On the basis of that final member, Irenaeus strongly reproved the heretics of his time, for he adds about them in c. 2: "When we reprove them from Scripture, we turn them into an accusation of Scripture as if they not be behaving correctly nor from authority and because the things they say, they say differently, because we cannot learn the truth [p. iii] from these people who don't know the teaching handed down from before. After all, the truth has not always been handed down in writing but orally. It was for this reason that Paul also said: 'We speak wisdom among the perfected.'" [1 Cor. 2:6]

Let someone compare for me these words of Irenaeus with the theological controversies of our time. He will find that this is not as much like comparing milk to milk and egg to egg as it is in harmony with those heretics which Irenaeus described. You see, Bellarmine writes that it is false that God commanded the apostles to write (Bk. 4, *de verb. Dei*, c. 3, col. 206); and that the proper and principal goal of Scripture was not to be the rule of faith but to be a sort of useful and instructive letter (same book, c. 12, col. 254); that we must believe many things which have not been written, and that Scripture therefore is not the total but a partial rule of faith (*ibid.*, col. 255). He also wrote that the apostles occasionally wrote epistles and that in those they dealt with disputations regarding dogmas only in passing (same book, c. 4, col. 212).

These and other statements injurious to God-breathed Scripture have been declared publicly (although, according to the definition of Gregory, *epist.*, it is "the letter of God Almighty, written to us and in which the words of God echo and in which we learn His heart."). Those statements are very closely akin to those of the ancient heretics unless we should wish to say [p. iv] that they clearly are the same as theirs.

That you not doubt us—even partly, at least—observe that the aforementioned "Atlas" of the Roman Church [i. e., Bellarmine] tries to prove the imperfection of Scripture and the necessity of traditions with the same argument which those ancient heretics used, for he writes in this way, Bk. 4, *de verb. Dei*, c. 8, col. 234: "Many mysteries of the Christian religion require silence. It does not befit Scripture that these receive an explanation in Scripture which the whole world reads. For this reason the apostle says, 1 Cor. 2[:6]: 'We speak wisdom among the perfected.'"

And yet, we have learned from Irenaeus and from the very beautiful outline of this statement that even those ancient heretics covered up their accusation of the imperfection with which they threatened Scripture.

What is even more wretched and strange, Bellarmine was not afraid to attribute to Irenaeus the ideas which Irenaeus attributes expressly to the original heretics, for he writes that way in Bk. 3, *de verb. Dei.*, c.8, col. 186. In Bk. 3, c. 2, Bellarmine teaches that people cannot settle controversies from Scripture alone because the heretics explain them in different ways. In Bk. 4, *de verb. Dei*, c. 223, he writes the following: "Irenaeus wants to extend tradition more broadly than Scripture, and one cannot attain the meaning of the more difficult Scriptures from Scripture but from tradition so that tradition is sufficient of itself." [p. v] Scripture, however, is insufficient.

However, it was not Irenaeus but those heretics who kept accusing Scripture of imperfection and appealing to traditions on the basis of that accusation. In this situation, Bellarmine adds his two cents worth to them, for he writes as follows, Bk. 4, *de verb. Dei*, c. 4, col. 213: "We must know that there are some truly divine books. We certainly can in no wise grasp this from Scripture. You see, even if Scripture should say that the books of the prophets and apostles are divine, nevertheless I would not believe this with certainty unless I shall have first believed that the Scripture which says this is divine. After all, we read here and there in the Islamic Koran that the very Koran was sent from heaven; and yet, we don't believe this. This teaching [of ours] is very necessary, namely, the fact that something is divine Scripture we cannot hold sufficiently from Scripture alone." (In Bk. 3, *de ecclesia*, c. 14, col. 188, he argues in this way: "To believe that the histories of the Old Testament or the Gospels of Mark and Luke are canonical Scripture and, in fact, that any writing is divine Scripture, is not absolutely necessary for salvation, for many have been saved without this faith.") *Ibid.*: "It is not enough to know that Scripture is divine, but we must know what that Scripture is, something we can by no means grasp from Scripture."

[p. vi] (In Bk. 1, *de verb. Dei*, c. 2, col. 4, he argues as follows: "Nothing is better known and more sure than Holy Scripture, which contains the prophetic and apostolic books. I conclude that nothing is better known and more certain than it. One cannot know that it is certain and well-known nor prove it deductively.") He goes on, *ibid.*: "We must not only know which books are sacred but also in particular that those which are in our hands are those sacred books, and this we certainly cannot hold from Scripture, etc." However, isn't this something which turns into an accusation of Scripture, as if it doesn't stand correctly and is not from authority, and because those who do not know the tradition cannot find the truth from Scripture?

In Bk. 3, *de verb. Dei*, c. 9, col. 190, Bellarmine writes as follows: "Scripture accepts various meanings, and it cannot say what its own meaning is. Scripture cannot interpret itself. Therefore it is not the judge of controversies of the Church nor is it sufficient to define them." But is not this, too, something which turns into an accusation of Scripture as if it does not stand correctly and because it speaks in various ways? However, the hinge (so to speak) of all controversies which arise between us and the teachers of the Roman Church—not only about Scripture but also about the rest of the articles—turns on the fact that we do not agree on the true and legitimate process for interpreting Scripture.

[p. vii] It is for that reason that I have quite often desired that our people make efforts to provide a careful explanation of this major point; for as often as we drive those light-shunners of Scripture (as Tertullian speaks, *de resurr. carnis*) with the decrees of the sacred tables, they just as often turn that head of Gorgon toward us and head for that unending refuge of theirs that the question doesn't concern Scripture and its majesty, but the true and genuine meaning of Scripture. That we must await from the Church herself—that is, from the Roman pope, who (and not we heretics) is the true Church. For that reason, we have suffered exclusion from the true understanding of Scripture.

Therefore, that I may offer our people a handle for pondering carefully this escape-route of our foes and for blocking against them all their loopholes for getting away, I desired to gather together on paper various thoughts of mine concerning this subject and allow them to become a public matter. I did not at all consider that I could not discuss this matter more carefully than by doing this myself; however, because of my insignificant talent and my weak work, I want to provide encouragements to others who have been equipped on a higher level than I that they themselves may be stirred to increase their support of the heavenly truth in this area.

[p. viii] To you, eminent gentleman, very noble in every way, I wanted to dedicate this little work of mine that I might gain some light for this small treatise from the august splendor of your name.

After all, who doesn't know or cannot know that you are noble in family and mind, in talent and ability, in art and warfare? Truly, you have wanted to consecrate the first years of the flowering of your life not only to your academic pursuits, but also to various travels to foreign places, and even to matters of warfare. I therefore admire that skill which you have in various disciplines and languages and your mental foresight which is prepared for all circumstances. I admire that skill in your counsels which you accommodate to both peace and war, as well as your authority in transacting negotiations with important people. Truly, no forgetfulness of ours nor of our descendants will ever erase that prudence of yours which was connected with your magnanimity which I saw at the Ratisbon Conference[2], when you dealt with the very honorable legate of the most illustrious dukes of Saxony!

I willingly pass over very many other occasions in which not only the eminent nobility of Franconia but also the most illustrious princes and electors waited for prudent counsel and immediate service in the absence of our energetic highness, [p. ix] and then very often experienced those when you were present.

I would heartily desire that you leave to us the inheritance of your most abundant fortunes and those high praises! But I recall that outstanding bon-mot which you at times would use in my presence and hearing, namely, that it was quite enough if it would appear good to God that that very ancient family line of the Selwitzes cease excellently in and with you. This would be better than leaving a son who perhaps was lacking in his paternal and ancestral virtue or who was not so energetic an imitator thereof.

Therefore, most noble gentleman, accept this small paper gift. Interpret it as a sort of indication of my grateful heart and as

---

2 The reference is to the 1601 Regensburg (Ratisbon) Conference, in which the Lutheran theologians (led by Aegidius Hunnius) debated with Roman Catholic theologians concerning the question of whether Scripture alone, without tradition, is the source and norm of doctrine.

a small kind of significance of my observance thereof, for you have conferred upon me so very many great benefits that I willingly admit that I am in their eternal debt.

May the Lord Jesus be present with us with His Spirit and grace to the end.

Written at Heldburg on 1 January of the year 1610.
With respect to your eminent sir,
Master Johann Gerhard

[p. x]
2 Corinthians 4:3–4:
*"But if this Gospel of ours be concealed,
it has been hidden in those who are perishing,
in whom the god of this world has blinded
the senses of those who do not believe,
lest the light of the Gospel of the glory of Christ,
who is the image of God, shine upon them."*

Augustine, On The Eight Questions of Dulcicius:
*"Because these words of the apostles are manifest and very clear testimonies,
they cannot be false. That which they may have spoken unclearly
we must understand in such a way that it not be found contrary
to these which are manifest."*

ON THE INTERPRETATION OF HOLY SCRIPTURE

[1]
Some things have been said quite obscurely in Scripture.[3]
¶1. We say that there is indeed such great clarity of Scripture that from it we can have some special and steadfast judgment about the dogmas which anyone must know for his salvation. In the meantime, however, some things therein have been said quite obscurely and as a consequence are quite difficult for man's understanding.

The use of that obscurity.
¶2. "Obviously the Holy Spirit has arranged Scripture so wonderfully and profitably that He remedies our hunger with the clearer passages but encourages our hunger with the more obscure ones" (Augustine, Bk. 2, *de doctr. Christ.*, c. 6). How accessible to all is the very manner of speaking which weaves together Holy Scripture, although very few penetrate it! [2] Those clear passages which it contains speak to the hearts of both the learned and the unlearned like a close friend. On the other hand, those things which it cloaks in mysteries do not. "It does not uplift with that arrogant eloquence which a somewhat sluggish and unlettered mind dare not approach like an impoverished person to a wealthy man; but it invites all people with its humble speech that it may not only feed them with manifest truth but also exercise them with secret truth. That the

---

3 Marginal notes in the original edition are usually included in the body of the text of the translation in this fashion.

clear passages not produce satiety, the same truth is desired in the unclear passages. When it is desired, it somehow becomes renewed and, when renewed, it is announced more sweetly" (the same, *Epistle 3, ad Volusianum*).

¶3. That obscurity of some passages of Scripture drives us to more ardent prayers, arouses our interest, wipes away our disinterest, commends the truth more, crushes our arrogance, summons the profane away from their knowledge of self, and stirs up reverence for the ministry which God has established among us.

How the ministry interprets Holy Scripture.

¶4. God indeed not only entrusts to us the very sacred deposit of His Word, but also has established among us the ministry of the Church, whose principal office is [3] to interpret Holy Scripture. "That is the ministry of the Spirit" (2 Cor. 3:8), "through which He desires to lead us into all truth" (John 16:13); "we therefore ought not quench the Spirit" (1 The. 5:19).

¶5. Thus Christ, in the form of a traveler, conversed with the men going to Emmaus and "kept interpreting to them the things which were written about Himself, beginning from Moses and all the prophets" (Luke 24:27). The same Christ, "sitting at the right hand of the Father, formerly not only gave prophets, apostles, and evangelists but also today gives pastors and teachers" (Eph. 4:11), "for the preparation of the saints, in His work of ministry, for the edification of the body of Christ" (v. 12).

¶6. Thus the account in Mat. 11 and Luke 7 about the sending of the disciples of John to Christ shows that in difficult questions about religion, we must not pass judgment on the basis of human opinions but should consult the mouth of Him about whom the Father said: "Listen to Him" (Deu. 18:18). He, in turn, sends us to Scripture (John 5:39), and from the words of Scripture He expresses His own response to the disciples of John in the same place. We must not on this account despise the ministry as disengaged and useless, but [4] Christ, once again setting forth the words of the prophets, sent His legates to John to use his work in examining the explanation of the statements of Scripture.

And this, according to the dictates of the Spirit.

❡7. Those ecclesial interpreters, regardless of the level of dignity on which they stand, ought not introduce any private meanings of Scripture but, as the sacred tablets were written from the inspiration of the Holy Spirit, so also they ought to explain them according to His dictates. For this reason, we declare that the Holy Spirit is the supreme and authoritative interpreter of Holy Scripture.

❡8. This we conclude clearly from the passage of the apostle, 2 Peter 1:20: "No prophecy of Scripture is born of private interpretation." Why? Because holy men of God formerly did not speak from their own private judgment but from the inspiration of the Holy Spirit (v. 21). Therefore, the same One who is the Author of Holy Scripture is the supreme and authoritative Interpreter thereof. He who creates a law is the best and supreme interpreter of the law.

From what source should we seek the dictates of the Holy Spirit?

❡9. Moreover, from this stems the question: What is "private interpretation?" From what source should we seek the dictates of the Holy Spirit in interpreting Scripture? How [5] can we know that those ecclesial interpreters are comprehending correctly the mind of the Holy Spirit as He speaks in Scripture?

The papists' claim from the Church.

❡10. The papists claim that we must attribute the following to the Church, namely, that she teaches clearly and infallibly what the true and genuine meaning is of Scripture, that Scripture in and of itself is a dead letter which one can explain in various ways and twist about in any direction like a wax nose, but that the Holy Spirit through the Church teaches us what the true and authentic interpretation is.

What they mean by "Church."

¶11. Too, because the hinge upon which the matter turns is this—that we therefore may perceive more fully their way of thinking—we shall relate what Nicholas Cusanus argues regarding this subject in his epistles against the Bohemians. From these we shall be able to understand what they mean by the honorable name "Church," what authority they attribute to her in interpreting Scripture, and, finally, what they claim is the infallible interpretation of Holy Scripture.

Cusanus

¶12. So then, Cusanus writes: "Some people say that in the first place we must obey the command of Christ. Next, we must obey the Church; and, if the Church may have commanded something other than what Christ may have commanded, we must obey not the Church [6] but Christ." (Next he adds a verification): "The beginning of all presumptions lies in this: when individuals judge that their meaning in the case of God's commands is more in conformity with His will than are those [interpretations] of the entire Church. He, however, remains in the Church who does not presumptuously elevate his own meaning about the dictates of the majority of the priests who have believed the Word and who are performing the ambassadorship of Christ. You see, in obeying that way of thinking which he sees the more sound part of the Church affirming, the Christian incurs no peril. The truth adheres to the bishop's office. The members, therefore, united as they are with the bishop's office and connected to the pope, make up the Church."

¶13. And later he writes: "We see that in the understanding of Scripture the varied inclinations of people explain varied ways of thinking and that a different opinion of the authority of Scripture exists and possibly will exist either in the author or the same people. We also see that in this understanding an irresolvable doubt suspends the thinking of people. Where, then, will we pilgrims find a solid refuge? Surely in nothing other than in the use and approval of the Church Militant, whether this is within Scripture [7] and its authority and understanding or lies outside Scripture in accepted custom through the Church. There is a firmness in these like a solid rock and pillar of the truth, not as if this proceeds to the Church through the authority of Scripture; nor can he reject this impunity if it is not in harmony with Scripture, and cling to Scripture. This is the way of thinking of all the truly intelligent people who base the authority or understanding of Scripture (as Augustine says about the Gospel) on the approval of the Church, which accepts the one and rejects the other. Too, it is not the way of thinking of those who conversely base the foundation of the Church on the authority of Scripture."

⁋14. On the basis of this foundation he responds to the argument of the Bohemians: "You perhaps will say: 'The Church of today does not walk in the ritual of communion in the same way as she did in times past when the very holy men of God used to affirm with their word and work that the Sacrament under both kinds was essential by virtue of the command of Christ. Could the Church have been in error at that time? Certainly not! But if she were not, how is this not true today which [8] in the opinion of all was being affirmed at that time, inasmuch as that Church was not a different one from that of today?' This surely should not upset you that in diverse times you find one and another ritual of the sacrifices and even of the Sacraments while the truth keeps standing firm, and that the Scriptures have been adapted to and understood according to the times, so that at one time the Church would explain them according to the current universal ritual and would change her mind at another time, etc. Therefore even today there may have been some interpretation of the Church of the same evangelical precept different from that of another time. This meaning, nevertheless, currently in use now was inspired for the management of the Church. We thus should accept it as in harmony with the times and as the way of salvation."

¶15. What sort of Church he means he explains later: "The universal Catholic Church which Christ has gathered at the throne of Peter will never pass away, for He is the truth, and He promised that He would remain with her always." He finally concludes: "On the bases of these premises, we agree that the entire Catholic Church cannot be bound to the letter of Scripture, for when the letter does not serve her edification and spirit, she accepts that which rather [9] serves her spirit. Therefore, it is not surprising if the practice of the Church at one time interprets Scripture in one way and at another time in another way, for the understanding runs hand in hand with the practice, and the understanding which runs along with the practice is the life-giving Spirit. The Church therefore receives Scripture just as she interprets it. Scripture therefore follows the Church which comes before it and for the sake of which Scripture is and not conversely." So much for Cusanus.

Hosius

Cardinal Hosius presents all these points briefly about the expressed Word of God: "If someone has the interpretation of the Roman Church, even if he neither knows nor understands whether and how it agrees with the words of Scripture, nevertheless he has the actual Word of God itself."

The Council of Trent

¶16. From these statements we can agree as to what the fathers of the Council of Trent wanted for themselves when in Session 4, Decree 2, they gravely forbade anyone to dare to interpret Scripture contrary to that meaning which the mother church had held and now holds, whose function it is to pass judgment on the true meaning and interpretation of Holy Scripture, or contrary to the unanimous agreement of the fathers.

Bellarmine

¶17. Let us see how Bellarmine [10] explains the thinking

of the Council. He says, Bk. 3, *de verb. Dei.*, c. 3: "We ought to understand Scripture with that Spirit who created it, that is, the Holy Spirit." The whole question therefore lies in this, namely, where is that Spirit? "We (papists) think that, although He has been conceded to many non-clergy, we certainly find this Spirit in the Church, that is, in a council of bishops whom the supreme pastor of the whole church has confirmed, or in the chief pastor along with a council of other pastors." From this he concludes: "The judge of the true meaning of Scripture is the Church, that is, the pope along with a council."

We ask two questions.

¶18. We cannot yet dismiss Bellarmine. Because he adds a council to the pope, we ask whether the holy Spirit then speaks directly through the pope when he along with or in a council of other pastors defines something or whether He also speaks then when the pope publishes a statement alone outside his council. In the second place, we ask whether in interpreting Scripture the authority of a council or of the pope is greater, for it is well-known that the pope and councils do not agree always.

[11] *The response of Bellarmine.*

¶19. Bellarmine responds to the first in Bk. 4, *de pontif. Roman.*, c. 2: "Infallibility itself does not lie in an assembly of counselors nor in a council of bishops but in the pope alone." To the latter, he responds in Bk. 2, *de concil.*, c. 13: "Catholics are not yet agreed about this matter." In c. 14, he presents three ways of thinking of (papist) professors: "Some affirm that a council is above the pope; others want the pope to be above a council but that a council cannot judge a pope against his will. However, they say that a pope can subject himself to a council and permit a council to pass judgment on his case. If he shall have done this, then he must acquiesce to the way of thinking of the council. Others, however, assert that the pope is so far above a council that he cannot even subject himself to its forcing way of thinking which it says is the common opinion, and follow the same."

They therefore defer the interpretation of Scripture to the pope alone.

¶20. From all these ideas, we draw the following conclusion. The papists claim that we must seek the true interpretation of Scripture solely from the shrine of the papal breast, for they are leading us from the authority of the Church to this ultimately through those long circumlocutions of their disputations. The wiser and more candid [12] among them will not deny this. Bellarmine therefore writes, Bk. 4, *de pontif.*, c. 2: "All Catholics agree on this: All the faithful must listen obediently to the pope alone or along with his special council when he claims something in a doubtful matter, whether or not he can err."

This truly is a multiple error.

¶21. This opinion contains far more errors. The original premise of this structure is false, because they separate the meaning of the Holy Spirit from the words of Scripture although they nevertheless ought not separate them and pull them apart but connect them very closely. The Holy Spirit speaks to us in and through Scripture. The voice and way of thinking of the Holy Spirit, therefore, sounds in those very words of Scripture. We are not to introduce any words from a different source into Scripture but must draw and hear meaning from those very words. To this belong all those declarations in which we read that the mouth of the Lord has spoken. They assert that "holy men of God spoke as the Holy Spirit moved them." For that reason, Scripture is God-breathed. The truth, in fact, is this: That all Christianity rests upon the foundation that the Holy Spirit made note of all the things we read in Scripture, and this through the prophets and apostles.

[13] ¶22. The papists clearly are presenting to us such an idea of Scripture which is, so to speak, a sort of skeleton and dumb and dead statue which must first be brought alive through the Spirit in and through the Church, that is, through the pope as he speaks. "The speech of God is alive and effective" (Heb. 4:12). Anyone may ponder how far this way of thinking of the papists is from Schwenkfeldianism, which also says that we must abandon the letter of Scripture as a dead item and follow our internal spirit.

¶23. The words of Scripture are the words of the Holy Spirit, whose mind they explain to us. We therefore must approach the reading of Scripture with that intention as if we are hearing the Holy Spirit speaking in and through them. You see, as the pope speaks to his people in his decretal letters, so also the Holy Spirit speaks to us in the divine utterances of Scripture. If anyone should wish to separate the meaning of the Holy Spirit from the words of Scripture, he will also have to separate that meaning of the pope from the words of his decretal letters. Thus no one today will be able to know what the first popes wanted for themselves. In fact, today's pope cannot express his way of thinking other [14] than through words. Therefore, if someone should wish to make the exception that these are indeed the words of the pope—but we must still ask about the meaning of the words and from what source we should seek that—he will deservedly laugh because the words are the marks of the senses of the mind. In the same way, the papists are absurd when they divide and separate the words of Scripture and the way of thinking of the Holy Spirit, for we must draw the meaning of the Holy Spirit from those words of Scripture and not introduce into them words from another source.

¶24. Let us make this matter clear. When Bellarmine and other papist writers try to show that we have withdrawn from the teaching of the fathers, they are always in the habit of repeating: "Jerome claimed this, Augustine thinks this, Ambrose speaks in this way, etc." I ask, however, how do they know that this was the way of thinking of Jerome, Augustine, Ambrose, etc.? Surely from their words, for they do not have anything else on the basis of which to respond. We speak in the same way, too: "The Holy Spirit claims this, thinks in this way, and speaks in this way." If they should ask from whence we know that this is the mind of the Holy Spirit, as if they wish to urge us [15] to draw the way of the thinking of the Holy Spirit from the voice of the Church, the Church, the Church; I say, if they should ask that, what else can we respond than that we must learn the mind of the Holy Spirit from the words of Scripture?

¶25. How, then, is our first point conceded, namely, that Scripture is God-breathed, and the prophets and apostles were the amanuenses of the Holy Spirit (something which no Christian, as a Christian, can deny)? One must also immediately concede that we must learn the mind of the Holy Spirit from that book and those words, and that there is no need to draw directly from the heart of the Roman pope what the mind and way of thinking of the Holy Spirit are. Lactantius asks, Bk. 6, *div. instit.*, c. 21: "Could not the Creator of mind and tongue speak clearly?" On the contrary, in fact, in His supreme foresight, He wanted those things which are divine to lack any disguise so that all people may understand what He Himself was saying to everyone.

¶26. Irenaeus says, Bk. 3, *advers. haeret.*, c. 1: "That very same thing which the prophets and apostles presented to their hearers—I say, the same thing and nothing else did they put into Scripture, and this they did by the will of God." In the same way, therefore, as the hearers of the prophets and apostles could perceive what the will of God and the mind and way of thinking of the Holy Spirit were [16] from their words; so also we readers of the prophetic and apostolic writers can perceive from their books what the will of God and the mind and way of thinking of the Holy Spirit are. Preaching and writing are external accidents which do not change the essence of a matter. As speech is the representation of the meaning of the heart, so writing is the representation of the words which the mouth presents. The philosopher[4] deals with this matter in περι ἑρμην, c. 1: "The spoken word is the symbol of the mental experience, and writing is the symbol of the spoken word."

¶27. Let us consider the fact that, when the pope intends to make known his way of thinking, he does not always use those very legates of his whom he has at his side to explain that aloud. He often merely sends letters of appointment and briefs (as they speak in his court). The person who hears these says that he is hearing the pope's way of thinking. In this way, the Holy Spirit formerly not only sent His prophets and apostles, who explained His mind in person, but even today He hands over to the Church the prophetic and apostolic writings in which the prophets and apostles, and through them the Holy Spirit, speak to us. Therefore, he who reads or hears these may claim that he knows the way of thinking of the Holy Spirit.

[17] ¶28. Let us come closer. The papist says: "We must learn from the Church alone, that is, from the pope, what the true meaning of Scripture is." I therefore ask what the source is for their proof of this papal privilege. They then provide various passages of Scripture from the Old and New Testaments, especially that statement of Christ: "I shall give you the keys to the kingdom of heaven, etc. Upon this rock shall I build the Church. I have prayed for you that your faith not fail, etc." (This you see in Bellarmine, Bk. 3, *de verb. Dei.*, c. 4 and 5.) They explain these words in this sense: that the promise about the infallible interpretation of Scripture was made to the Roman throne and to the pope who sits upon it, and that he is always going to obtain the genuine meaning of the Holy Spirit in those words. What if I should entertain doubts about that interpretation of the statements of Scripture as to whether I must

---

4 i.e., Aristotle.

accept them in his sense? In what direction will the pope lead me away? Surely to the shrine of the papal breast. What an egregious confirmation! This privilege of not erring befits the pope, for he interprets the passages of Scripture in such a way that it befits him to reveal that. Also, we must understand those passages of Scripture that way because the pope wanted us to understand them that way.

[18] ¶29. But who of the fathers do you see interpreting Scripture in this way, namely, this the true and genuine explanation because the Roman pope has published it? And why do the Jesuits today want to appear that they are debating very carefully from Scripture by consulting the sources, comparing passages, etc.? They will be able to conclude the entire matter briefly if they should say: "People must believe these articles and we must explain Scripture in this way because the pope has defined them in this way." Obviously the pope is cautious in this office of his. He certainly ought to have made authentic some interpretation of Scripture of either Lyranus or someone. Otherwise how will one know what properly is the interpretation of the Roman pope?

¶30. Surely the Roman pope attributes and allows people to attribute to him the great privilege of interpreting Scripture! But he should show us the official documents and seals, I say, the divine statements, indicating that. Perhaps we shall be able to discover it in the document in which the donation of Constantine[5] is written that we may examine more carefully its outer part, as was once advised by the Venetians in a different case, according to Camerarius, part 1, *medit. histor.*, c. 61.

¶31. The ideas which the Jesuits produce today to confirm that privilege [19] they have sought for an excessively long time, and they always take them from: "In the beginning...," for they deal with

---

5 The reference is to the fraudulent "Donation of Constantine" which papists claimed was an imperial decree made by Emperor Constantine which transferred temporal authority to the pope. The fraudulent character of the document was revealed in the mid-fifteenth century.

either the Church in general or with Peter by relating them to the chief priest of the Old Testament. However, they cannot produce any testimony which clearly mentions the pope. In the matter of privileges, there ought to be a clear and expressed testimony of him to whom God granted such great things, for the Jesuits teach that this should be done. The special treatment of those passages which the Jesuits produce in this argument belongs to the article of Roman faith concerning the pope.

¶32. In addition, let us see how the pope has used this great petition (if it ever was conceded to him), and how cleverly he has interpreted Scripture. The Jesuits, you see, teach that the benefits granted through privilege have been lost through abuse. The theme is quite common in the *decret. pontif.* For example: "The prince and secular judge must not accuse nor condemn bishops and priests," something which Clement (*epist.*, 1) proves from the fact that Paul says: "It ought to be of very little concern to us that we reprove on the basis of such things or on the basis of a special human day."

Anacletus

Anacletus (*epist.*, 1–3) proves this [20] from the fact that Christ says: "He who touches you, touches the pupil of My eye"; that Peter writes: "God resists the proud but gives grace to the humble" [1 Peter 5:5]; that John advises: "that "we not believe every spirit" [1 John 4:1]; that Paul asserts: "Each will render an account for himself" [Rom. 14:12]; that the Lord—not through someone else, but Himself—with a whip cast out of the temple the priests who were buying and selling; that the royal psalmist said: "God stood in the synagogue of the gods ... and all of you are the children of the Most High," [Psa. 82:1 and 6], and because Paul asks: "Who are you who are judging another's servant?" [Rom. 2:1]. Telephorus proves therefrom that the Lord denies that the disciple is above his master.

Siricius and Innocent

❲33. Thus Siricius (*epist.*, 4) and Innocent (*epist.*, 3) try to prove that marriages of priests are illicit because we read: "Be holy, because I too am holy" [Lev. 11:44], and: "Those who are in the flesh cannot please God" [Rom. 8:8]. If a priest has been contaminated with carnal lust, with what shame of conscience will he sacrifice or with what merit does he believe that God will hear him, because it is written: "All things are pure for the pure, but for the defiled and unbelieving nothing is pure?" [Titus 1:15]. (See also c. *decernimus*, dist. 28; c. *proposuisti*, [21] dist. 82; c. *tenere*, dist.31; etc., and Vol. I, *concil.*, f. 422.)

How Anacletus proves the primacy of the Roman Church.

❲34. Anacletus proves that the Roman Church has received from the Lord primacy and the eminence of power over all the churches and of the flock of the whole Christian people, and this from the fact that Christ said to Peter: "You are Peter, and upon this rock (that is, the Roman see) I shall build the entire Church" [Mat. 16:18]; that Paul says that he mentions the memory of the Roman Church in his prayers without ceasing; and that the Lord conceded to Peter that he be in charge of the rest of the apostles; and that, as Cephas, he hold the headship and lead of the apostolate.

Innocent

❲35. Thus in c. *solitae. extra de majorit. et oboed.* (which the *glossa* says is very citable), Innocent III wants to prove that the empire is bound to obedience to the priesthood, because God said to the priest: "Behold, I have set you over the nations and kingdoms to tear down and scatter, to build up and to plant" [Jer. 1:10]; and also: "God placed two great lights in the firmament of heaven" [Gen. 1:16 and 17]; that is, He set up two great offices in the Church which are the pontifical authority and the royal power; but, as great a difference as there is between the sun and the moon, so great a difference is there between popes and kings.

[22] Boniface VIII

❡36. In that same renowned chapter (as the interpreters call it), Boniface interprets Scripture in this way: "When the disciples said, 'Behold, we have two swords here,' [Luke 22:38] namely, in the Church, the Lord does not respond here: 'That is too much' but: 'That is enough.' In the Church, therefore, there are two swords, namely, spiritual and temporal.' Also, the Lord says to Peter: 'Put your sword back into its sheath.' The temporal sword, therefore, lies in the power of Peter."

We can gather very many such explanations in the *decretales pontificum* in which the popes do not *interpret* as much as *ravage* Scripture. They are not explaining it but are imposing upon people through it. By this very fact, they are showing that they have abused most woefully the privilege of interpreting authoritatively that in this way they have lost it, even if the Lord might have conceded any such thing to them.

❡37. What, however, is this incorrect use of language and unnatural license that those decretals understand the pope alone by the name "Church?" One person isn't the Church, is he? Will they be able to produce from Scripture a proof of this possibility? On the basis of this hypothesis, the pope is the vicar of Christ, the successor of Peter, and the head of the Church. We nevertheless must not take [23] "Church" to mean him alone for those reasons. How destructive are the frauds which that Roman ape, clad as he is in the honorable cloak of "the Church" so that everything which we read about the Church in Scripture we must relate to the pope alone or at least primarily to him alone! Why do the papists use those circumlocutions to name the Church and mean only the pope?

❡38. On the contrary, in fact, if the pope is the chief and authoritative interpreter of Scripture, it will follow that we must assign to him the immediate and infallible assistance of the Holy Spirit and then, consequently, we must equate his decrees and interpretations with the prophetic and apostolic writings. After all, whatever the immediate inspiration of the Holy Spirit produces will be equivalent to the prophetic and apostolic utterances.

The fabricated authority of the pope.

❡39. Why, then, don't we offer to the pope—along with those fabricated legates of Gabriel, the patriarch of Alexandria—such writings in which the following titles are prefixed: "To the father of fathers," "To the prince of the patriarchs," "To the thirteenth apostle," "To the fifth evangelist," "to the successor of St. Peter"? (See *Suscitab.*, part 1, c. 16, *ex Dousa.*) Why don't we cry out to him [24] what we read in the Bernard of today, Bk. 2, *de consid. ad Eug.*, col. 1023: "You are the prince of the bishops, you are the heir of the apostles, by the primacy of Abel, by the governance of Noah, by the patriarchate of Abraham, by the order of Melchizedek, by the dignity of Aaron, by the authority of Moses, by the judiciary of Samuel, by the power of Peter, by the anointment of Christ."

Why don't we conclude long with Gratian, c. *in canonic.*, dist. 19: "We should count the decretal letters of the pope among canonic Scriptures," which opinion Gratian attributes criminally falsely to Augustine, as if he is teaching such a thing in Bk. 2, *de doctr. Christ.*, c. 8, although this did not enter the mind of Augustine. Bellarmine (Bk. 2, *de Concord.*, c. 12) acknowledges the crime of Gratian but in the meantime, he softens it in such a way that he says that Gratian was deceived by a corrupt manuscript of Augustine. He finally concedes that, in their own way, the decrees of the popes are and can be called "holy and canonic Scripture."

Why don't we, along with Angelo Politiano (from his *orat pro Senen.*) address the pope in this way: "Most blessed father, we congratulate you that, elevated to the summit of human affairs as you are and, in fact, clearly conveyed to divinity itself, may you see all things except God as lesser than yourself [25] and inferior to yourself, so that even the very kings and princes worship your footprints and do not disdain licking the dust from your feet but even aspire to the place of this outstanding duty."

¶40. It is common practice among papist writers to transfer the things which Scripture declares about the chief priest of the Old Testament to the Roman pope. I no longer argue that point with just right for we know that in the Old Testament God Himself appointed some man as the high priest and that this priest was a type of Christ, as the Epistle to the Hebrews teaches. However, in the New Testament we acknowledge no other chief priest and high priesthood except Christ. As I said, I no longer argue about this point, but I do ask this: No authoritative and absolute authority for passing judgment on and interpreting Scripture has been given that priest of the Old Testament, has it? Not at all. Rather, Moses established the divine Law as the norm of judgment (Deu. 17:11). It alone, however, does not claim such great authority; but a judge is summoned to participate in the same (v. 12). Therefore, as a political judge ought not depart from the norm of public laws in passing judgment regarding political cases, so also a priest ought not stray from the norm of [26] the moral and ceremonial laws in passing judgment on ecclesial matters.

Cardinal Cajetan, as interpreter, has changed this passage, for in the Hebrew we read "or to a judge." Here a prudent reader should know that the settling of ambiguous cases is reached not by a single person but by many priests and a judge. The carrying out of a sentence is assigned either to a priest or to the judge, etc. (See Jerome, *ab Oleastio*, on this passage.) Judges are not free to pass judgment as they wish but according to the laws; and people must obey them when they have passed judgment according to them.

¶41. Where, however, do we read that the doctrine which the prophets and apostles used to preach was examined by their devout hearers or was commanded to be examined to search out the meaning of the chief priest? Isaiah complains, 56:10: "All His watchmen are blind. They all are ignorant." Jeremiah cries out, 6:13:"From the prophet all the way to the priest they are all lying." Ezekiel complains, 7:26:"The Law will perish from the priest, and good advice from the elders." At times, the book of the Law has been considered of such [little] worth that, for a long time it had been lost, but under Josiah it was discovered again (2 Kin. 23:2). [27] Malachi (2:7) connects "right" and "deed":"The lips of the priest guard knowledge, and people seek the Law from his mouth." (This is about one's right.) V. 8:"But you have strayed from the way; you have offended many in the Law; you have corrupted the covenant of Levi, says the Lord of hosts." (This concerns the deed.) Wouldn't this have been an egregious interpretation of prophetic interpretation, had the people kept asking for their meaning?

¶42. Thus, at the time of Christ and the apostles, the chief priests, and the entire senate of the ecclesial nobility were condemning the teaching of Christ and the apostles, as we agree from the digests of the account of the Gospel. Of what character, therefore, would the interpreters of apostolic teaching have been, had the people consulted them? Because the apostles and prophets put into writing later the same things which they had preached, therefore we conclude the following: If some authoritative and absolute power of passing judgment over the true meaning of prophetic and apostolic preaching did not befit the chief priest of the Old Testament whom God Himself had elevated to that level of sublimity; all the less will the Roman pope be suited for such great power [28] by which he can pass absolutely authoritative and simply infallible judgment concerning the true meaning of the doctrine included in the prophetic and apostolic writings.

¶43. The prophets used to appeal "to the Law, to the testimony" (Isa. 8:20). Christ would invite His hearers to "search the Scriptures" (John 5:39), and the apostles encouraged theirs to "consult Moses and the prophets," outside of whom they kept protesting that they were saying nothing (Acts 26:12). The Holy Spirit recommended to the Bereans that they search Scripture daily, examining whether the preaching of Paul and Silas was in harmony with it (Acts 17:11).

That statement of Christ: "The scribes are seated upon the throne of Moses, etc."

❡44. Christ indeed says (Mat. 23:3) that we must keep and do whatever the scribes have said as they sit upon the throne of Moses. However, that no one thinks that He is attributing to them some absolute privilege of passing judgment on and of interpreting Scripture, He therefore elsewhere (Mat. 5:7 and 23) reproves them with great frankness for their false teachings by which they kept closing the doors of heaven to people. He also warns them (Mat. 16:6) to be careful of "the leaven of the Pharisees and Sadducees," that is, of their corrupt teaching, as He explains clearly in v. 12. Those words, then: "The scribes and Pharisees are sitting upon the throne of Moses [29]. Whatever they may have said to you, keep and do," we must take as repetitive, namely, in this way: "… to the extent that they sit upon the throne of Moses, that is, to the extent that they teach those doctrines which are in harmony with the teaching of Moses. But if they teach some things from the throne of pestilence and corrupt the sincerity of Mosaic teaching with their leaven, to that extent you must not listen to them."

Biel (Bk. 4, *sent.*, dist. 1, q. 4, art. 3) writes: "We must not reject the counsel of the prelate, because it is true unless he will have spoken contrary to divine Law, because by commanding such things he is not sitting upon the throne of Moses. After all, such matters do not proceed from the throne, that is, from the teaching, of Moses but from the throne of pestilence."

Wessel, who lived around 1455, wrote: "We must observe the commands of prelates so long as they sit upon the throne of Moses and teach according to Moses. If they teach anything contrary to or outside of Moses, we are not bound thereto, for we are the servants of God and not of the pope."

A summary of the arguments against the papists' way of thinking concerning the interpretation of Scripture.

¶45. Let us summarize what we are claiming in the matter of the papists' way of thinking about the true interpretation of Scripture. First, they are considering separately the way of thinking of the Holy Spirit as if we must seek the Holy Spirit's way of thinking from a source different [30] from the words of Scripture. Second, they claim that Scripture is a dead letter which the spirit of the Church must enliven. Third, they claim that there is a real distinction between that which the prophets and apostles preached and that which they later put into writing, as if their preaching would have been understandable, but that we must draw an understanding of their writings from a different source. Fourth, they take the word "Church" to mean one pope. Fifth, they attribute that authoritative privilege of interpretation to the pope without Scriptural support. Sixth, they are compelled to accept absolutely the absurd interpretations and accommodations of Scripture which we read in the decretal letters of the popes. Seventh, they attribute to their pope the prerogative which we owe to the prophets and apostles alone. Eighth, they attribute to him such a great thing which befits not even the chief priest whom God Himself appointed. Ninth and finally, they are compelled to make the final resolution of their faith the shrine of the papal breast. But, the historical accounts which note the words and deeds of the popes bear witness how impure that has been sometimes. Mat. 12:33: "The mouth speaks out of the abundance of the heart."

[31] We must seek the true interpretation of Scripture solely from the Word of God.

¶46. "On what basis," you ask, "can we be certain about the true interpretation of Scripture? We must not pursue some personal spirit in interpreting Scripture, must we? Will not some action drive you to confess that in some passages Scripture is unclear and in need of interpretation? From what source must we draw that? Is it not more satisfactory for the whole Church to usurp this authority to interpret than to concede to each person license to follow his own spirit? Did not Jerome speak very truthfully in his commentary on Gal. 1: 'Let us not think that the Gospel is in the *words* of Scripture but in its *sense*; not on its *surface* but in its *marrow*; not on the pages of its discourses but in the root of reason?' From what source, therefore, must we draw its meaning?" As Bellarmine says, Bk. 3, *de verb. Dei*, c. 9: "Scripture cannot tell what its true meaning is. Scripture cannot interpret itself. All the heretics appeal to Scripture, and they all boast that they have the Spirit." The papists repeat these and similar complaints speciously and pompously. To them we respond as follows.

¶47. All knowledge is involved between the subject one must know and the understanding intellect, because understanding is the acceptance into the intellect of a species from an object known abstractly. [32] The action of the acting intellect follows this, as Scaliger argues about this matter (*exercit.*, no. 307, sect. 21). What is required, then, between the recognizing intellect and the object to be recognized is a correspondence (*adaequatio*), just as in a vision which is, so to speak, a shadow and model for the intellect.

¶48. Because the mysteries of faith which Scripture sets forth are divine and have proceeded from the direct revelation of God, therefore they surpass the sphere of our intellect which sin has so woefully corrupted, if I may speak in this way. 1 Cor. 2:14: "The natural person does not perceive the things which are of the Spirit of God. They are foolishness to him, and he cannot understand them." Accordingly, they require beyond the natural powers and original riches of our intellect the illumination of the divine light. Otherwise the mysteries which Scripture has presented will remain a closed and sealed book.

According to Luther, what requires the illumination of the Holy Spirit?

¶49. As a result, Dr. Luther (*de serv. arbitr.*, Bk. 3, Jena edition, p. 167) says: "Not even a single letter in Scripture is clear without the light of the Holy Spirit, for all things are unclear to the flesh and acumen of man in this area and respect." Indeed, light has been left to our reason [33] by which we can use philosophic disciplines and some part of the divine Law for reproving external sins in comprehending and examining earthly matters. However, our reason is utterly blind to comprehend the divine mysteries in Scripture. In fact, even if Scripture may present them openly, nevertheless we cannot have a salutary and solid knowledge thereof without the internal illumination and light of the Holy Spirit. From this source the distinction between the knowledge of the letter and of the spirit trickles down.

Prayers therefore are necessary.

¶50. We must pray for this divine and spiritual light of the Holy Spirit, for "the Holy Spirit is given to those who ask for Him" (Luke 11:3); "The Son, who is in the bosom of the Father, reveals the mysteries of our salvation to us" (John 1:18). In turn, "No one comes to the Father, unless the Father Himself draw him" (John 6:44). Therefore we must pray that the Father draw us to the Son. We must pray that the Son reveal the Father to us. This is the anointing which teaches all things (1 John 2:27). "The Spirit is the One who leads to all truth" (John 16:13). Therefore we must pray the Holy Spirit that He Himself write in our hearts and there seal those things which are presented outwardly in the Word.

[34] ¶51. This illumination of the Holy Spirit is necessary for interpreting and understanding all Scripture and any part thereof in salutary fashion. Any readers and interpreters of Holy Writ, therefore, must pray seriously: "O Lord, let me not stray from Your commandments" (Psa. 119:10). "Teach me your statutes" (vv. 12, 26,

64, 68, and 124). "Open my eyes, and I shall consider the wondrous things of Your law" (v. 18). "Give me understanding that I may learn Your commandments" (vv. 73 and 125, etc.).

¶ 52. Irenaeus writes, Bk. 4, c. 14: "The pious ancients knew this." We do not know God without God, something which the Christian poet[6] expressed in this way:

"Stop wondering why no one sees God without God!
Who sees the sun without the sun?"

Origen writes, homily 17 on Exodus: "We must beseech the Lord that He Himself deign to take the sealed book and open it, for it is He who opens minds to understand Scripture." Jerome (*ad Pammach.*) also says that Scripture is a sealed book which no one can open nor unlock its secrets except the Lion of the tribe of Judah. We therefore must pray the Lord and say with Peter: [35] "Explain to us that parable." Theophylactus writes, commentary on John 10: "Because Scripture presents, opens, and shows Christ to us, the Holy Spirit is justifiably the Doorkeeper."

¶ 53. We shall relate to this the prayer of Augustine which is in Bk. 11, *confess.*, c. 2: "My Lord and my God, be attentive to my prayer, and may Your mercy hear my desire. May Your Scripture be my pure pleasure. Let me not be deceived in it, nor may I deceive from it. O Lord, heed me and have mercy upon me. O Lord my God, the Light of the blind and Strength of the weak as well as the Light of those who see and the Might of the strong, pay attention to my soul, and hear it crying from the depths. If Your ears be not present also in the depths, where shall we go? Both day and night are Yours. At Your nod, the moments fly by. Grant us, therefore, time for our meditations on the hidden matters of Your Law. Do not close it against those who are knocking at its door. After all, You didn't want so many pages of its secrets to have been written in

---

6 Iacobus Lectius/Jacques Lect (c. 1556–1611), denounced as a Lutheran in the Papist *Index Librorum Prohibitorum*.

vain. Look, my Father! Look, see, and approve. May it be pleasing in the sight of Your mercy that I find grace before You that [36] the inner secrets of Your words be disclosed to me as I knock. This I beseech You through our Lord, Jesus Christ, Your Son. I beseech You through Him who sits at Your right hand and intercedes for us and in whom are hidden all the treasures of wisdom and knowledge. It is He whom I seek in Your books. Moses wrote of Him. He Himself says this; the very Truth says this."

¶54. Furthermore, what we have said up to this point about the illumination of the Holy Spirit which is necessary for us to comprehend Scripture we want to be understood especially about the mysteries of the faith which have been set forth in Scripture. Although some things have been so arranged in Holy Scripture that they do not exceed the grasp of human intellect (briefly, the outer bark of historical accounts), nevertheless the human mind cannot ascend by force of its native light to comprehend solidly and salutarily the mysteries of the faith without the illumination of the Holy Spirit. Indeed, those whom the Holy Spirit has not yet enlightened can become acquainted with the dogmas of Scripture and have an external faith through the external ministry of the Word; they cannot, however, have a certain assurance and a solid and salutary knowledge thereof without [37] the Holy Spirit illuminating their minds internally.

The necessity of the illumination of the Holy Spirit is no argument in favor of the obscurity of Scripture.

¶55. The need to seek the illumination of the Holy Spirit is necessary because of the darkness of our intellect. This, however, is no argument in favor of the obscurity of Scripture in presenting the mysteries of faith. Bellarmine and other papist writers who keep busy proving their way of thinking about the obscurity of Scripture on this basis are acting rudely. The eyes of the blind do not perceive even the brightest objects and therefore do not see the sun itself; but who would wish to attribute darkness to the sun for that reason? In the same way, our intellect is so darkened that it does not perceive the mysteries of faith which Scripture has presented in clear and lucid language; but who would therefore wish to attribute this darkness to Scripture itself?

The clarity of Scripture.

¶56. On the contrary, in fact, we are so far from attributing darkness to Holy Scripture for the reason that we rather contend that we must attribute to it the power to enlighten our intellect, because the Holy Spirit enlightens our minds through Scripture itself. This is something which all those declarations prove [38] which compare the Word of God as presented in Scripture to light, whose property is to illuminate; for instance, Psa. 19:9: "The commandment of the Lord is clear"; Psa. 119:105: "Your word is a lamp for my feet and a light for my path"; Pro. 6:23: "Your commandment is a lantern and Your law a light"; and 2 Peter 1:19: "The prophetic word is a shining light in a dark place." Just as natural light repels darkness, so also the spiritual darkness of our intellect is illumined through the light of Scripture, for which reason Paul attributes illumination to the Word of God (2 Cor. 4:4).

¶57. We are saying, then, that the light of the Holy Spirit is required for the salutary interpretation of the divine utterances. We do add, however, that through our diligent handling of the Word, the Holy Spirit wishes to kindle that light within us. We should not think that we should await from the Holy Spirit an immediate illumination from on high before we go on to reading, meditating on, and carefully examining Scripture. Rather, we must pray for and obtain that light of the Holy Spirit in and through Scripture. That's why St. Peter used to say: "We must pay attention to the prophetic word as if it be a lamp shining [39] in a dark place until the day (of divine perception) dawn and Lucifer (Christ, the Morning Star, Rev. 22:16) rise in our hearts."

¶58. Obviously Scripture presents those things which anyone must know for his salvation in appropriately clear and lucid language, as we have shown in its own place. Therefore, to understand and interpret those, we do not require some external light or some long-sought interpretation. Rather, the Holy Spirit speaks lucidly and clearly in those areas. Through such passages, He wishes to dispel the natural blindness of our intellect.

The very aggressive blindness of some.

¶59. As the very bright shining of the sun places things in a clear light, so the natural blindness of our minds is driven away through this light of Scripture. In addition to that inborn and inherent darkness of our mind, there is also another very aggressive blindness of some people because of which they reject that light of the Holy Spirit and freely turn their eyes away from it, as if someone freely and knowingly closes his eyes to the illumination and enlightenment of the sun. The Lord speaks about this blindness in Isa. 6:20: "Shut the eyes of this people, etc."

[40] ¶60. Likewise, we must not conclude on the basis of this blindness and hardening of the wicked that in its teaching of the mysteries of the faith Scripture is obscure and in need of an external light, just as we should not conclude that because some people close their eyes that the light of the sun not appear to them. Therefore, to gaze upon the light of the sun, we require another illumination. 2 Cor. 4:3–4: "If our Gospel has been hidden, it has been hidden in those who are perishing, in whom the god of this world has blinded the minds of the faithless that they not see the light of the Gospel of the glory of Christ."

The rule of faith.

¶61. From these very clear passages of Scripture, we glean the rule of faith which is a sort of summary of heavenly teaching which we gather from the very clear passages of Scripture. It has two parts. The first concerns the faith whose principal topics the Apostles' Creed explains. The latter concerns love, a summary of which the Decalogue explains. 2 Tim. 1:13: "Hold tightly the form of sound words which you have heard from me in the faith and love which are in Christ Jesus."

¶62. Chrysostom therefore says (homily 3 on 2 Thessalonians) that whatever things are necessary have been revealed in Holy Writ. If any subjects are unclear in it, an understanding thereof accordingly is unnecessary [41] for the salvation for all people. Thus, even if we may not always reach the genuine and appropriate interpretation of those passages, nevertheless it is enough that in our interpretation thereof that we not produce anything which is opposed to the rule of faith. Rom. 12:6: "(We must conduct prophecy) according to the proportion of our faith."

¶63. We therefore must be careful in our interpretation of the less clear passages not to produce anything which conflicts with the constant and eternal sense which is comprehended in clear words in Scripture about each main point of celestial doctrine, for all Scripture is "God-breathed." For that reason, all things in Scripture are "consistently true with each other." There is nothing contrary here, nothing in conflict, nothing disagreeing with anything else.

The remedies for, and the sources of, obscurity.

¶64. Those more obscure passages of Scripture are such when we either take them by themselves and separately from others or compare them with others. For, when we consider many of these by themselves and separately from others, they are quite clear but nevertheless appear to conflict with other statements of Scripture. You see, although there is no true conflict in Scripture, an apparent contradiction of passages does bring with it a sort of lack of clarity. We remove discrepancy from Scripture, [42] but we cannot deny an [apparent] contradiction of some passages. Thus, what the Lord says in Eze. 18:20 is quite clear: "The son will not bear the iniquity of his father." A sort of obscurity is brought to that from the passage Exo. 20:5: "I Jehovah am a jealous God, visiting the iniquity of the fathers upon their children to the third and fourth generation." For this obscurity a connection of the passages which we must draw from the circumstances and conform to the analogy of faith provides a remedy.

Another obscurity comes from taking passages by themselves and separately.

¶65. Passages which we take by themselves and separately from others may suffer an obscurity either because of their situations or because of their words. You see, there is a permanent connection of subjects and of words as things signified or as signifying. Consequently, if the subject matter is unclear, we attribute the lack of clarity to what is said or written, even if the words are clear. In turn, if the words are unclear, we attribute the obscurity in like manner to what has been said or written, even if the subject matter is well-known and clear.

The lack of clarity of subjects.

¶66. The enlightenment of the Holy Spirit provides a remedy for the obscurity of subjects because without it the articles of faith remain unclear and a closed and sealed book. The subjects or mysteries of faith are presented in two ways: in some places [43], catechetically, that is, briefly, simply, and generally (a manner of teaching which Scripture calls "milk," 1 Cor. 3:2 and 2 Heb. 2:12 and 13) and elsewhere in detail, splendidly and specifically (which teaching it calls "solid food"). The school of Aristotle would call the latter "acroamatic" [or "abstruse"] but the former "esoteric." To avert this lack of clarity which is produced from subjects, it is quite useful to hold onto certain axioms in any article of faith, which axioms we always respect as our polestar lest we relate something contrary to some article in our interpretation of Scripture.

Obscurities of words.

¶67. That lack of clarity which we attribute to the words of Scripture is twofold. The one is born from words which we take individually; the other, from those same words when we connect them together. You see, as words taken separately are insufficient for some discourse or treaty but must be joined together and connected appropriately that they become declarations; so also, for the understanding of some discourse or treatise, we must understand not only the words as we take them separately but we must also understand the same when we have connected them with each other.

[44] Obscurities of word taken separately.

¶68. The obscurity produced from words when we take them separately from each other is twofold, for words are either specific or figurative. The grammatical explanation of words and an observation of their emphases help to understand and to interpret specific words. Here if any careful interpreters of Scripture examine carefully where the same word is used in other passages of Scripture, they will detect that this is by far the greatest use of this comparison and observation. You see, whether that word is used in the same or in a different sense, always observing this is the basis of theological study and of the faith of the interpreter of Scripture. Rhetoric also serves the explanation of tropes and figurative language.

¶69. Scripture uses metaphors and parables which it takes from the innermost depths of nature. The knowledge of natural things is especially advantageous for explaining them. After all, who will interpret appropriately those parables of the Savior about yeast, mustard seed, a vine, etc. without having a precise or at least a common perception of the natural properties of these?

Obscurities of words connected together.

¶70. If connected words cause Scripture some lack of clarity, [45] this is born from either the phrasing or from the entire nature of the discourse. Not only the grammar but especially the prudent and careful comparison of passages of Scripture serves the understanding of Scriptural phrasing. An observation of the order and circumstances helps one understand correctly the entire context. Pertinent to the observation of the order is the dialectic observance of the goal and parts of the discourse. The circumstances which we can relate to these main points are varied: occasion (cause, intent), times, place, manner (instrument). We can subdivide all these still further. For instance, with reference to person we must consider who is speaking, to whom he is speaking, the subject of the speech, in whose presence it is spoken, etc.

A summary of our statements about the true interpretation of Scripture.

❡71. Let us reduce to a summary what we are claiming about the true interpretation of Scripture. First, in understanding and interpreting Scripture, our mind is blind, absent the light of the Holy Spirit. Second, in addition to the native blindness of us all, some people whose eyes the Holy Spirit did open or wanted to open suffer blindness because of their own malice and obdurate peevishness. Furthermore, they obstinately resist the Holy Spirit. [46] Neither blindness, however, causes Scripture to be unclear. Third, because our mind is blind, we must pray for the light of the Holy Spirit. Fourth, the Holy Spirit, however, does not grant the illumination of our mind without means but through the light of the Word which we hear and upon which we meditate. Fifth, because anyone must know dogmas for his salvation, Scripture presents these in appropriately clear and lucid language. Sixth, it is from those passages that the rest of the passages of Scripture provide light. Seventh, it is indeed from the clear passages of Scripture that we conclude the rule of faith to which we must conform the explanation of the rest of Scripture. Eighth, even if we do not reach the proper and genuine meaning of all the passages, it still is sufficient that in interpreting them we provide nothing contrary to the analogy of faith. Ninth, it nevertheless is useful to interpret even those more obscure passages of Scripture correctly and skillfully, something which will occur if we should apply the appropriate remedies for resolving obscurities. Tenth, that we may discover those remedies, we must seek out the sources of the obscurity. Eleventh, some passages are unclear of themselves and considered separately; some, when they are compared with other passages. Obviously, when they appear to conflict with other passages, [47] a connection of passages remedies this lack of clarity. Twelfth, passages which are obscure of themselves and when taken separately we detect are such either because of their subject matter or because of their words. Some specific axioms in individual articles of faith provide a remedy for this obscurity, and these we must observe as our polestar. Thirteenth, serving to resolve the obscurity of words are a grammatical explanation of the words, a rhetorical exposition of the tropes and figurative language, and finally a physical understanding of natural subjects. In fact, prudent and diligent comparison of passages of Scripture will offer the greatest assistance, for there we may apply the same or different words and phrases to express the same or different subjects.

⁋72. We have said these things in general about the means which we require for the legitimate interpretation of Scripture. We say that the greatest and most authoritative interpreter of Scripture is the Holy Spirit, who sets forth in appropriate and clear words in Scripture the dogmas of faith which are necessary to anyone for his salvation. However, for the skillful interpretation of those passages which are quite unclear in Scripture, we also [48] require prayers, a knowledge of the language which the amanuenses of the Holy Spirit used, an observance of the order and circumstances in any passage and a prudent and diligent comparison of passages. We say especially that we must pay zealous attention to the rule of faith that we not produce anything contrary thereto in our interpretation of the more obscure passages.

The papists' means of interpretation.

¶73. We shall deal more specifically with all these later when we shall have first explained what means the papists present to us. You see, in place of the greatest and most authoritative Interpreter they establish their pope and thus substitute other means which we ought to use in our interpretation of Scripture. Stapleton addressed this subject at some length, Bk. 11, *princip. fid*, and in his *relect.* of the same, controversy 7. Let us listen to him.

According to Stapleton.

¶74. He proposes four means by which we can arrive at the true meaning of Scripture. The first is the rule of faith; the second is the practice of the Church; the third, the unanimous interpretation of the fathers; and the fourth, the prescripts and decrees of councils. He says that these means alone [49] are certain and authoritative. Let us therefore look at these individually. Later, whatever he produces contrary to our means we shall place on the scales of the truth.

1. The rule of faith.

¶75. Stapleton requires the rule of faith. We also require the same rule but in a clearly different sense. "On the one hand, we say the same words, but on the other hand we understand different things." We take "rule of faith" to mean clear passages of Scripture which present the articles of faith in clear and lucid language. To this are related all those arguments by which we proved in its own place that Scripture is perfect and clear and consequently the canon of all theological controversies.

¶76. Furthermore, because the greatest and most special points of this rule are presented in the Apostles' Creed, the fathers therefore call that creed "the rule of faith." When Irenaeus explains the rule of faith (Bk. 1, *adv. haeres.*, c. 2), he goes back to the Apostles' Creed. Tertullian says, *de veland. virg.*: "The rule of faith is indeed totally and alone immovable and unalterable, namely, for believing in the one God, the omnipotent Creator of the world, and in His Son, Jesus Christ, born of the Virgin Mary, crucified [50] under Pontius Pilate, on the third day He rose again from the dead, ascended into heaven and sits at the right hand of the Father, and who will come to judge the living and the dead also through the resurrection of the dead." Augustine writes, *enchirid.*, c. 56: "If the Holy Spirit were not God, He would not be set before the Church in the rule of faith." Ambrose says, sermon 38: "The apostles gathered together for this one things, namely, to prescribe the rule of faith."

❡77. In these citations, the authors call the Apostles' Creed "the rule of faith." Because, however, each and every one of the chief points which it presents is set forth in clear words in Scripture, they themselves call Scripture elsewhere "the rule of faith." Irenaeus (Bk. 4, c. 69) calls the Word of God "the rule of truth." Clement (epistle 5) says that we must seek the full and firm rule of truth from divine Scripture. Augustine (*de bono vid.*, c. 1) establishes Holy Scripture as "the rule of our teaching"; and in *contra Donatist.*, c. 6, he calls Holy Scripture "the divine measuring stick." In Bk. 11, *de civ. Dei*, c. 33, he writes: "Although we have been unable to examine the will of the author of this book, I have not strayed from the rule of faith which the faithful have known quite well from other sacred writings of the same authority." Chrysostom (homily 13, [51] on 2 Corinthians) calls Scripture "The most precise balance beam, measuring stick and rule of all." Gerson, *de comm. sub utr. spec.*, says: "Holy Scripture is the rule of faith against which we must not admit the authority of humans when Scripture is well-understood."

❡78. The papists propose another rule of faith. They add to Scripture traditions which they claim we must embrace with an equal feeling of devotion. This rule, however, is very irregular, as we have shown in its own place. Scripture is the total and perfect rule to which we must not add anything and from which we must not take away anything. Accordingly, if traditions are in harmony with Scripture, we accept them; if, however, they disagree therewith, we justly reject them.

2. *The practice of the Church.*

¶79. The second means was the practice of the Church. We shall show, however, in its own place that we must not subject Scripture to the Church. What the true Church is and what the true and salutary practice of the Church is—all this we must learn from Scripture. The prescript, practice, and right of customs does not run on divine paths, for Christ did not say: "I am the custom," but: "I am the truth."

¶80. Therefore, as the papists don't take a stand on [52] the practice of the Church, but merely approve and follow the practice which the pope has confirmed (something which an analysis of the papist way of thinking shows), so also with far greater right we do not take a stand on the bare practice of the Church but ultimately approve and follow that practice of the Church which has its foundation in Scripture. Briefly, for the papists what the pope pronounces from his throne is for us the Holy Spirit speaking in Scripture.

¶81. The papists say that their hearers ought to follow their pastors. In turn, the pastors must follow their bishops, but the bishops themselves must follow the instruction of the pope. So also we say that their hearers should follow their pastors, but their pastors should follow the instruction of the Holy Spirit in Scripture which has proceeded from God.

¶82. The papists say that in the interpretation of Scripture we must follow the rule of faith, the practice of the Church, the agreeing interpretation of the fathers, and the decrees of councils. We do not disapprove of these means. However, just as they themselves add that we must embrace the rule of faith of which the pope approves, the practice of the Church which the pope observes, [53] the interpretations of the fathers which the pope ultimately does not reject, and the decrees of those councils which the pope confirms; so also they should allow us to add that the true rule of faith is that which Scripture proposes, the true practice of the Church is that of which Scripture approves, the true interpretation of the fathers is that which is not opposed to Scripture, and the true decrees of councils are those which are in harmony with Scripture. Augustine writes, Bk. 11, *contra Faustum*, c. 5: "Canonical Scripture has been established on a sort of a most-high throne which every faithful and devout intellect must serve."

3. The harmonious interpretation of the fathers. 4. The Decrees of the councils. What we should think about the interpretation of the fathers.

❡83. The third means was the harmonious interpretation of the fathers; the fourth, the decrees of councils. We shall have to speak about councils in their own place. Let us not despise the interpretations of the fathers but rather magnify them. Nevertheless, we should not make them equal to, nor prefer them to, the declarations of Scripture. Rather, we defer such high honor which the former usurp for themselves to that which the Truth attributes to the latter.

❡84. We proceed. First, the papists themselves deny that the authority of the fathers is always [54] absolutely authentic. Baronius writes, Vol. 1, *anno* 34, ❡213: "It is clear with how little grace the Holy Spirit has imbued the very holy fathers whom we call 'doctors of the Church' because of their lofty erudition; for in her interpretation of Scripture and in all other things she does not always follow them." Bellarmine, Bk. 2, *de concil.*, c. 12: "The writings of the fathers are not rules nor do they have authority to bind." Pereira (*in Genes.*, Bk. 2, c. 2, q. 5) affirms that the elders of Asia who were the disciples of the apostles accepted what he taught about Paradise, but what happened then later? Must we consider whatever those elders taught as the sure and undoubted dogma of Christian doctrine? Do we not agree that those very elders, as the same Irenaeus relates, taught some things which were false and contrary to Holy Writ?

Canus (*Bk. 7, loci theol.*, c. 3) testifies that the fathers erred often. Cajetan (preface on *libr. Mos.*) asks that he not blamed if at times he disagrees with the verbal floods of the fathers. Stapleton (*relect. princ. Fid.*, contr. 6, q. 4) in his explanation of the article says: "We must distinguish what the fathers in passing sometimes write and when they act differently from those things [55] which they handle intentionally and principally; for the former cause great faith while the latter create very little. We must also distinguish the things which they said once from what they affirm and repeat steadfastly and often. Especially we must distinguish those things which they teach dogmatically and assertively in a substantive treatise from those which they declare in disputing a contentious battle against an adversary, even in a matter of faith. From this latter type of statements we must take no testimonies, because in those it easily happens that one goes beyond the limit and transgresses the limit of the truth." So much for Stapleton, as he himself keeps the interpretations of the fathers within specific bounds.

¶85. Second, they use boastful words about the consensus of the fathers. The situation actually shows this. You see, they do not agree in every detail on dogmas, nor in the interpretation of Scripture. That we not appear to be speaking too freely, we shall confirm this with one or two examples. The psalmist says, Psa. 66:12: "We have passed through fire and water, and You have led us into a cool place." Origen (homily 25 on Numbers) accommodates this passage to his purgatory, [56] and the papists follow this. Do the fathers unanimously interpret this passage in that way? We shall run through some.

Arnobius (or whoever the author was of those commentaries), on Psa. 65 (for the Latins number them in that way), understands it as a reference to the fire of martyrdom and the water of Baptism. Cyril (*catech.*, myst. 5) understands this as pointing to the passing through of temptation. On this passage, Augustine explains "fire" as a reference to adversities and "water" as the abundance of the age. Hilary explains it in the same way. Euthymius takes "fire and water" to mean the calamities which set fire to and drown the soul. So does Theodoret. Ruffinus explains it as temptations; Haymo, about martyrs whose courses neither fire nor water could hinder; Bede, about various tribulations. In a sermon on his translation of Malachi, Bernard interprets "fire" as a reference to tragic matters and "water" about gentle matters, as does Cassiodorus, on the same passage. Lyranus accommodates the passage to the slavery of the Israelites in Egypt: "We have passed through fire, that is, through the hardship of fire for 'cooking,' and the water which they used to carry [57] on their own shoulders to mix with dirt to shape bricks therefrom." But these aren't harmonious interpretations of the fathers, are they?

❡86. What the apostle says in Rom. 7:14 ("I am carnal, sold as I was under sin."), Jerome, Athanasius, and Ambrose interpret in such a way as if Paul there is not speaking about himself but in the persona of a person not yet reborn. However, Augustine (Bk. 2, *contra Julian*, c. 2, and elsewhere) confirms that we must understand this as a reference to the apostle himself. Thus, when Paul says, Rom. 3:28: "We maintain that a person is justified by faith without the works of the Law," there Ambrose takes the word "person" as a reference to the heathen alone, while Chrysostom takes it to mean all people. Jerome takes "works of the Law" to mean ceremonies; while Ambrose and Augustine understand it as a reference to the entire Law, etc. We could bring up very many more such points.

❡87. Third, for this reason the papists subject the interpretations of the fathers to the Roman pope. In this way, Bellarmine (Bk. 3, *de verb. Dei*, c. 3) establishes the pope along with his council as the supreme interpreter of Scripture, and therefore argues (Bk. 2, *de concil.*, c. 12) that one can be correct in calling the decrees of the popes "Holy Scriptures" to distinguish them from [58] secular writings, and "canonic" to distinguish them from the sacred writings of the fathers but that these are not rules nor do they have binding authority.

Stapleton (Bk. 10, *princ.*, c. 11) says that we must accept the interpretation of bishops and the teachers of the Church under the following conditions: first, only if they will have remained in Catholic unity, that is, if they have been submitted quietly and peacefully to the authority of the pope; second, if they will have agreed with their co-bishops, etc. Pistorius (*hodeg.*, p. 51) says that the interpretations of the fathers become valid then finally when the Church will have approved of them; that is, the Roman pope, as the final analysis teaches. Thus the Roman Catholics subject the authority of the fathers to the pope. But with what greater right do we subject it to Scripture?! Let there be those whom we call "fathers." Let us be their children. When they prescribe something from the Law and divine authority, let us obey them as our parents. If they prescribe anything contrary to the norm of heavenly teaching, let us obey God and not them. Let them be and be considered as lights and not deities.[7]

⁋88. Fourth, what has been so arranged that we must not always interpret as a rule of Scripture, [59] and what has not always had the authority of an authentic judgment—that very thing ought not even have the force of a rule or judgment. Indeed, "it is required that a rule be one thing, certain, firm, and changeless." The harmonious interpretation of the fathers has not always been the rule for interpreting Scripture, for at some times there were no writings of the fathers. Few of them wrote before the four hundredth year after Christ. Therefore there will not even be a rule of Scripture then.

---

7 *lumina et non numina*

¶89. Fifth, Stapleton requires for "the unanimous consensus of the fathers" that they agree with all their fellow bishops, but from what source can we know this? After all, there were many other bishops of those times, none of whose books or writings survive. On what basis will we have a sure agreement that Augustine, Ambrose, and others agreed with all their fellow bishops?

¶90. Sixth, how much work would it take to run through the universal writings of all the fathers that we may finally be certain about the harmonious interpretation of those who wrote? And what span of human life would be equal to this work? But now, the norm of judgment and truth in the Church must be set up in such a way that any Christian may be able to run back to it. [60] Indeed, it is incumbent upon them all to test the spirits (1 John 4:1), and to be careful of false prophets (Mat. 7:15).

¶91. Seventh, the fathers themselves remove such authentic authority of passing any such judgment and of interpreting Scripture, something which we can elicit from very many places. How many times does just one, namely, Augustine, distinguish the canonic excellence of Holy Scripture from the insignificant works of later writers? See Bk. 11, *contra Faust.*, c. 5; Bk. 2, *contra Crescon.*, c. 32; Bk. 2, *contra Donat.*, c. 3, epistle 19, to Jerome' epistle 48, to Vincentius; epistle 112, to Paulinus. The following repeat the same thing: Jerome, commentaries on Psa. 86, Micah 2, Isa. 19, Eze. 36, etc.; Basil, *de S. S.*, c. 7; Origen, on Rom. 2; Athanasius, *Syn.* See also c. *Noli*, c. *Neque*, c. *Ego solis* and c. *Negare*, dist. 9.

¶92. Eighth, not all the books of those fathers who wrote are extant, and the ones that do exist quite often have been corrupted. Many spurious ones were written and produced [61] under the venerable cloak "books of the fathers," and many also experienced the censuring *Indices*.[8]

¶93. Ninth, in the heat of debate, the fathers sometimes

---
8 The *Index Librorum Prohibitorum*—that is, the Romanist *Index of Forbidden Books*.

spoke inappropriately. (Basil, epistle 64, *de Greg. Neocaes.*: "What he said, namely: 'The Son and the Father are a single substance[9],' he said not on the basis of a decree but as a slip of the tongue." Erasmus passes the same judgment about Jerome as he wrote *contra Vigil.*)

"In exhorting, we orate too heatedly." Thus wrote Jerome, as he excused some things he said inappropriately: "We orated and produced something in our blustering." Sixtus of Siena (Bk. 6, *bibl. annotat.*, note 152) advises: "We should not always take the words of preachers with the same strictness by which they first reach the ears of their hearers, for they often speak and teach many things through hyperbole, moved as they have been by the occasion of places, persons, and times, or caught up by the force of their emotions or the course of their speech." Theodoret (dial. 3) concludes that this sometimes happened to Chrysostom: "I do not think that the things which speakers say in a panegyric and declamatory way are a rule of dogmas and decrees."

"They spoke more calmly before battles erupted." [62] (Thus Augustine, Bk. 1, *contra Julian.*, c. 2, acknowledges that, when the Pelagians were not yet quarreling, the fathers spoke quite carelessly, *de liber. arbitr et peccat. orig.*) "They allowed anything in their own times." Augustine speaks in this way (epistle 119). In order to avoid the offenses of some people who were either saints or violent people, he approved too freely of some words. Canus, Bl. 11, *loci commun.*: "We cannot deny that some people, who otherwise were most serious especially in writing down the portents of the gods, made exceptions of rumors that had been spread and related them for their descendants in their books. In this matter, they either indulged themselves excessively or certainly indulged the common folk among the faithful."

Sometimes they speak recitatively and historically and not dogmatically (Otto Frising., Bk. 4, c. 18: "We must consider in what

---

9 ὑπόστασις

respect the authors are speaking in giving their opinion or in asserting something."), and, as a result, the later fathers explain the statements of the prior ones according to the analogy of faith, or they simply reject them if they are unable to reconcile them therewith. Augustine clearly refutes that which appears in Justin, Irenaeus, Clement, and Tertullian, namely, that the heathen have been saved by the law of nature. He also explains, according to the analogy of faith, the things which the Pelagians were publishing [63] in favor of establishing the innocence of free will.

¶94. Tenth, the fathers did not write with the purpose of illuminating Scripture with some new, external light, but of being of service to the people and controversies of their own time. They therefore confess that they had drawn their words from sacred writings and were interested in proving all things from them.

¶95. Eleventh, many of the fathers lacked a knowledge of languages, and for this reason they were unable to grasp the proper meaning of each passage. Someone should read Augustine's explanations of the psalms. He will then see how far people had strayed from the Hebrew truth. Most of the fathers pursued a more copious manner of speaking, especially case and rhyming endings, than scrupulous considerations of the text and grammatical explanations of words. Many touch on the literal meaning only slightly and soon stray off to allegories. Who consequently will rest upon the interpretation of the fathers?

¶96. Twelfth and finally, the papists have not yet proved that our churches, either in dogma or in their interpretation of Scripture, [64] have rebelled against the unanimous confession of the fathers. There is no dogma of our confession, no chief point of controversies, for the confirmation of which we cannot provide many clear testimonies of the fathers. In turn, our adversaries will be unable to offer a unanimous and harmonious interpretation of the fathers by which to prove papal indulgences, the invocation of the saints, the veneration of relics, works of supererogation, and other controversial dogmas.

¶97. These, then, are the means of interpreting Scripture which the papists are foisting upon us. Let us tell the things which we do not simply reject. We say, however, that we have submitted these to the authority of Scripture. We contend that the rule of faith has been presented in Scripture. We do not reject the practice of the Church, the ways of thinking of the fathers, or the decrees of councils, provided they receive their force from Scripture; for our faith should not be revealed in the way of thinking of either the fathers or councils but in Holy Scripture, for "we are built upon the foundation of the prophets and apostles" (Eph. 2:20). Also, [65] we acknowledge Christ as the only supreme and authoritative Teacher (Mat. 23:8), whose voice resounds in Scripture. Let us see what they bring forth against our means.

What the papists bring forth against our means.

¶98. First, the papists dispute in this way. First, they say that these means of ours we have in common with all heretics—in fact, even with Jews, and sometimes with pagans. After all, they also compare passages of Scripture, consider antecedents and consequences, examine the sources, and observe phrasing. Nevertheless, they cannot be farther from a true understanding of Scripture. This is the way Stapleton and the rest of their writers deal with the subject.

¶99. We respond. If they are saying that these are 'means' in this sense that they are also common to all heretics and pagans, and that all people can use them, we concede what they are bringing into the argument. After all, God speaks to all people in Scripture, and He desires that all read and become familiar with it and hear Him in it. However, if they say that these means are common to all in this sense, that they actually and legitimately use them and are proving their own heresies through them, then we say that this is absolutely false. We concede their right to use them, but we deny that they actually do use them. [66] In the interpretation of Scripture, no one has ever strayed through the legitimate use of these means. We shall be able to sufficiently refute heretics, Jews, and pagans on the basis of Scripture which we have interpreted through the legitimate use of these means, something which the writings of our people prove clearly. The person who does not rest upon Scripture, that is, upon the way of God as He speaks through Scripture, all the less will he rest upon the opinion of the fathers, councils, or the pope!

¶100. Second, they say that they really are people who use those means; in the meantime, those means are and remain divine. You see, the passages become clearer, and from them the obscure become clearer and are the utterances of the Holy Spirit.

¶101. The antecedents and the consequences are declarations of the Holy Spirit. The Hebrew and Greek sources contain the words of the Holy Spirit. The style and phrasing are the speech of the Holy Spirit. Next, we place in charge of the use of these means the schoolmastering of the Holy Spirit for which we must pray [67], as well as the analogy of faith, that is, the voice of the Holy Spirit as it echoes in clear passages. Therefore, when Bellarmine argues in Bk. 3, *de verb. Dei*, c. 3 and 9, that we are leading people off to each person's own personal spirit, note this carefully: If some ordinary person passes judgment from the clear passages of Scripture on some controversy of religion, this does not proceed from a personal spirit but is the public judgment of the Holy Spirit as He speaks in Scripture. In turn, even if a person established in a public office of the Church produces anything in the articles of faith beyond and outside of Scripture, that has proceeded from a personal spirit, even if he be the pope or some lofty bishop.

¶102. Panormitano (c. *Significasti*, extr. *De elect*) says: "We must believe an ordinary faithful person who offers better reasons than an entire council and the pope." Gerson, *de exam. doctr.*, cons. 5: "As regards some ordinary person who had no [ecclesial] authorization but who had received excellent learning in Holy Writ, we must find his assertion more credible in a doctrinal case than a declaration of the pope, for we must believe the Gospel rather than the pope." [68] Marsilio de Padua (*defens. pacis*) writes: "In matters concerning faith we must prefer a statement of even one ordinary layperson to a statement of the pope, if it be brought from better authorities of the Old and New Testaments than of the pope." Giovanni Pico della Mirandola, *de fide et ord. cred.*, theorem 16: "We must believe a simple hillbilly, an infant, or a little old lady rather than a very great pope and a thousand bishops if they speak against the Gospel while the former speaks words in favor of the Gospel."

⟪103. Their means, however, are truly human and only probable; for their rule of faith, to the extent that it includes traditions, is uncertain and doubtful. It also includes materials of people. The papists instituted very many things which they are peddling as things which God has handed down, as Platina[10] and Polydorus Virgilius[11] testify. The Church is an assembly of human beings; councils are gatherings of human beings. The fathers were human beings. The pope is a human being (unless we perhaps should wish to declare briefly along with the *Gloss, cum inter nonnullos, extra de verb. sign.*, "The pope, our lord god," or, with the gloss in the *proem.* of Clement on the word "pope" that he is a sort of medium between God and humans). [69]. The Church, councils, the fathers, and the pope can err, if their Teacher, the Holy Spirit, does not keep them under control. That schoolmastering of the Holy Spirit is either an immediate impulse of the Holy Spirit such as existed in the case of the prophets and apostles or a receiving of direction through the leadership of Scripture. We cannot say the first, for otherwise,

---

10 that is, Bartolomeo Sacchi (1421–1481), who wrote *Vitæ Pontificum Platinæ* (*The Lives of the Popes*).
11 that is, Polidoro Virgili (1470–1555), who wrote *De Inventoribus Rerum* in 1499, adding five additional books to the work in 1521 on the origins of Christian rites and institutions.

the decrees of the Church, councils, fathers, and the pope would be equal to prophetic and apostolic Scripture. Therefore, the latter remains and, as a consequence, Holy Scripture is the rule of the Church, councils, fathers, and the pope.

¶104. Third, they are saying that those means of ours are completely subject to those which they themselves present and have no firmness except insofar as ours agree with theirs. You see, unless from an observance of the antecedents and consequences, from a comparison of passages, from an examination of the sources, etc., they pluck some such sense which is in harmony and congruent with the rule of faith, the decrees of councils, and teaching of the holy fathers, we judge that their means are deceitful and harmful.

¶105. We respond. First, we admit that those means of ours are subject to the rule of faith. That rule of faith, however, is presented in clear and lucid passages of Scripture. On the other hand, [70] they want to be obedient to a rule of faith which is broader than Scripture. Second, they demand that we must accommodate to our means the practice of the Church, the decrees of councils, and the opinions of the fathers to Scripture, but not against Scripture, and this as if to the norm, which would subject the voice of God to the declarations of God. Third, the practice of the Church is changeable and often faulty. Neither councils nor fathers settle all controversies or interpret all the passages of Scripture. In fact, the later fathers often disagree with the earlier ones, and later councils also disagree with earlier ones.

¶106. Fourth, consequently, the papists themselves subject all these means of theirs to the Roman pope, for they approve that practice of the Church which the pope observes, they approve of the decrees of councils over which the pope has presided or which he has certainly confirmed. They accept the opinions of those fathers of whom the pope has approved. We subject all these much more correctly to Scripture. This will not be opposed to the true Church, to true councils, to the true fathers—for these have always subjected all those things to Scripture.

¶107. Fifth, we therefore say that in the interpretation of Scripture [71] we ought not depart rashly from the practice of the Church, the decrees of councils, and the opinions of the fathers. If, on the other hand, Scripture itself—that is, the voice of God sounding in Scripture—should command something different, who would not prefer listening to God to listening to people? So, too, in the examination of the sources, if the observation of the antecedents and consequences, as well as a comparison of passages along with statements of the New Testament show that Augustine in his commentary on the Psalms did not arrive at the genuine meaning of a passage, who might produce with the aid of these means the true and genuine meaning better than Augustine? Augustine himself commanded this, when he says in the introduction to Bk., 3, *de Trinit.*, that he desires "not only a pious reader but also a frank corrector."

¶108. Sixth and finally, because the Romanists subject the pious and diligent study of Scripture to the practice of the Church, councils, and the fathers, and, in addition, subject all these to one pope, someone may justly say with Erasmus, in his notes on 1 Cor. 7, p. 373: "If that is true what some are declaring, namely, that the Roman pope can never err in an error of judgment, why do they need general councils and why do they need to summon into council [72] experts in the Law and learned theologians if he cannot slip when he speaks? Why do they give to a name the place for a synod or someone who has received a better education after the pope has once made a pronouncement about a case? Why does it happen that so many academies become upset in dealing with questions of faith when they may hear what is true from one pope? In fact, contrariwise, how does it happen that the decrees of this pope conflict with decrees of that one? After all, this is something which many examples prove."

Against the observance of antecedents and consequences.

€109. The papists argue these points in general against our means. In particular, against the observance of antecedents and consequences, Stapleton urges the following: that sometimes this may be a great help, but nevertheless it is an uncertain and deceitful means. First, the context of Holy Scripture is not an unbroken discourse or methodic proof. Instead, in the same context, we have a mixture of historical, mystical, and figurative matters. Second, the order of speaking in Scripture is very often interrupted, sometimes irregularly. It is especially frequent in the case of Paul that he suddenly passes over from one subject to another. Third, in one and the same sentence some words are said in their strict meaning, and in another in a loose way, etc.

[73] €110. We respond. We are not presenting this one means as if it be sufficient for the explanation of all passages of Scripture. Rather, we are saying that in some passages this means prevails best, in others, the examination of the sources and in still others a comparison of passages works best. In our estimation, it works very well for us if we arrive at the true meaning of Scripture by using all those means. Although we may not arrive at the genuine meaning of some passage as accurately as possible, nevertheless, we will not stray from the rule of faith. We therefore do not disapprove of what Stapleton brings up from Augustine, Bk. 1, *de Genes ad lit.*, last chapter:"We must select that means especially which the circumstance of Scripture does not hinder and which agrees with sound faith. If we cannot deal with and discuss the circumstance of Scripture, at least this alone holds firm which sound faith prescribes." This is absolutely true, but Augustine neither establishes nor seeks that rule of faith in the shrine of the papal breast but in Scripture itself, as we have shown earlier.

The examples of Stapleton which he has produced as proof.

¶111. The examples which Stapleton produces with which to prove that this is a slippery and uncertain means [74] we can explain easily by applying the other means which we are presenting. In fact, this very means is absolutely powerless in the case of those latter. Thus, when we read in Gen. 3:7 that the eyes of our first parents were opened when they had eaten the forbidden fruit, the antecedents show that we must take this figuratively, for there we read (v. 6) that Eve saw that the fruit of the tree was pleasant to see. A comparison of passages explains what we read in Psa. 22:1: "My God why have you abandoned me? The words of my sins are far from me." You see, in Mat. 27:46, Christ bears witness that this is His statement and complaint. An examination of the sources explains the latter words, for they had to be translated in this way: "You are far from my salvation. My roaring is far from words."

Thus, we read in John 1:10: "The world was made through Him, but the world did not know Him." Here in the first part we must take the word "world" literally, but metaphorically in the latter, something which the antecedents and consequences as well as a comparison of passages show: "All things were made through Him" (v. 3); "God said, etc." (Gen. 1:3); "By the Word of God were the heavens made" (Psa. 33:6). So then, the world was made through the Son. "The light came into the world, and people [75] loved the darkness more than the light" (John 3:19). "The light shines in the darkness, and the darkness did not comprehend it" (John 1:5). "He came to His own, and His own did not accept Him" (v. 11). "Whatever is in the world is the lust of the flesh, the lust of the eyes and the pride of life…" (1 John 2:16). "The devil is the prince of the world" (John 14:30). So, then, the world does not recognize the Son.

The following verses show that what we read in John 4:35 ("Lift up your eyes and see the fields for they are white for the harvest") is something we must take figuratively as a reference to the spiritual harvest, v. 36: "The person who harvests receives his reward and gathers fruit unto eternal life"; and v. 38: "I sent you to harvest that in which you did not work."

¶112. If, however, our means are insufficient to explain those passages, I ask: What help will traditions, councils, the practice of the Church, the judgment of the pope, and the explanation of the fathers offer us in the explanation thereof? We obviously must hope for nothing from traditions and councils in this area. How many popes, on the other hand, [76] were not even acquainted with the seat of these passages, much less their genuine meaning?

Against the observation of phraseology.

¶113. Stapleton proves that we can establish nothing certain from an observation of phraseology in the following way: (1) first, because the individual writers of both the Old and the New Testament have their own way of speaking. Isaiah, who was reared in the royal court, speaks in one way; Amos, a shepherd, speaks in another way; Paul speaks in a way different from that of Peter, etc. We say that this process of and by itself is insufficient for explaining all the passages of Scripture. Sometimes it is sufficient only to assist us. Plutarch relates how king of the Scythians, on the day of his death, presented to his sons whom he was leaving behind himself a bundle of eighty spears and commanded each to break the bundle. Each, however, said he was unable to accomplish that. Then he himself took apart the bundle and easily broke the spears one by one. He then advised them that they would be strong and powerful if they remained steadfast as a single group, but that they would be weak if they separated one from another and disagreed. Stapleton is behaving in the same way. He is unable to break our means when they are bundled together; therefore, he tries to break them individually. He battles on the basis of tricks. [77] He should be attacking these means of ours as military companies joined together; but he is attacking them when they are divided one from another.

¶114. We readily admit what he says about the variety of ways of speaking, but we add that we can observe and learn thoroughly that variety with careful study. All the prophets and apostles spoke on the basis of the inspiration of one Holy Spirit. They had one Schoolmaster for speaking. Amos did not learn what he was saying from shepherds, nor did Isaiah learn what he was saying from the court, but they both learned from the Holy Spirit. But the popes aren't explaining that dissimilarity on the basis of their decretal letters, are they? The councils didn't learn that from their decrees, did they? The fathers perhaps explain it, but aren't they themselves very different in their own styles?

¶115. (2) Stapleton brings up another point against the observation of phraseology, and that is that the variety of interpreters or even of the original writings produces an uncertainty about the phraseology and manner of speaking. You see, a phrase observed according to a version from the Greeks will have a different suggestion [or flavor] observed according to a version from the Hebrew. We respond. We therefore add to this means the examination of the sources, for they do not have so great a variety. [78] The New Testament contains many Hebraisms which we must learn from Hebrew phraseology. If there is a variety of phraseology in the very sources, we can become acquainted with them from a prudent comparison of different passages far more correctly than from the corrupted fabrications of the rabbis or from interpreters who are ignorant of the Hebrew language. This is something which Förster confirms very clearly in the preface to his lexicon.

¶116. (3) The third point which Stapleton urges against the observation of phraseology consists in this, namely, that in the very rules and observations of this kind there is nothing certain and changeless, but each rule and observation produces many exceptions. We respond. Therefore, because the rules are not absolutely general, will they consequently be useless? We must draw from Scripture those very rules and exceptions which we add to the rules. Here the popes also can rarely provide assistance, for rarely have they been learned in Greek or Hebrew. Therefore, Stapleton is trying to prove that we cannot establish a general rule that "the eyes of the Lord" signifies His mercy and that "the face of the Lord" signifies His wrath, because we may also take "face" to mean His kindness in other passages. But for what purpose does he bring up these examples? [79] Obviously, to prove that rules about the ways of speaking are not absolutely general. However, Scripture itself teaches this very thing, namely, that it is enough that some rules can have a sort of generality if we ever must add some exception to a rule. In this way, therefore, one mean serves another. A comparison of passages assists the observation of phraseology, the rule of faith restrains the comparison of passages, etc.

Against a comparison of passages.

⁋117. Stapleton proves that the comparison of passages is a very deceptive and uncertain means of interpretation in the following way: (1) first, because in a comparison of Scriptures, something appears to be said either similarly or dissimilarly not so much on the basis of the similarity or dissimilarity of the passages themselves as on the basis of a feeling and prejudged way of speaking of the very passages. We respond. We require an interpreter who approaches this subject without prejudice and that he not introduce into Scripture his own meaning or preconceived opinions, but that he draw the truth from Scripture and not force the statements of Scripture to appear to contain that which he presumes he must understand before he reads the passage, as Hilary speaks, Bk. 1, *de Trinit.*

⁋118. On the contrary, in fact, from what source otherwise than from the circumstances of each passage can we learn whether a comparison of similar and [80] dissimilar passages is legitimate and sound? What help can the fathers (who also at times compare passages less skillfully) offer here? What help can councils provide, for they don't employ that comparison? What about the pope, who makes pronouncements from his throne and on the basis of the fullness of his power? The person who is unwilling to assent to Scriptures when someone compares them correctly and skillfully will be all the less moved by a statement of the pope. Furthermore, we are not saying that we must pick up this means alone and of itself and subject it to the rule of faith. For example, Stapleton brings up the words of the Supper ("This is My body"), but he says that there is no agreement about those; rather, that these have been woefully corrupted as a result of a comparison of different passages. Bellarmine also presses the same point (Bk. 3, *de verb. Dei*, c. 9). We shall deal with this subject a little later, however.

¶119. (2.) Next, Stapleton brings this up against the comparison of passages, namely, that neither the same wording nor the same phrasing sound and mean the same thing everywhere. We respond. From what other source can we learn this, save from an actual examination of each passage and from the circumstances thereof? [81] Therefore, it is useful not only to compare passages among themselves which are similar in phraseology or subject but also which are different in either phraseology or subject, for the parallel ones are most obvious. We can understand and explain the various meanings of any one word better from no other source than from a comparison of passages.

¶120. (3.) Third, that is because some passages are said only once in Scripture, such as being buried with Christ, being crucified with Christ, living with Him, ruling together with Him, etc. We respond. We are not saying that there is a use for this means in every passage. The things which are said only once as regards their very words are nevertheless repeated elsewhere as regards their actual subject matter. Also, they are either clear, or an understanding thereof is less necessary for us to know. The actual context of the apostle's discourse explains very clearly what the apostle means with regard to being buried together with Christ, being crucified with Christ, living together with Him, ruling together with Him, etc. In addition, he explains the same ideas elsewhere with other words.

¶121. (4.) His fourth point is that, in comparing Scriptures very carefully, all heretics have erred most shamefully. We respond. This is an insult against the divine pages that a skillful and careful comparison of Scriptures is the cause of error, [82] because Christ declares the opposite, namely, that ignorance of Scripture is the source of errors for heretics (Mat. 22:29). But how does Stapleton prove his declaration? He says: "The Arians compared that statement of Christ: 'I and the Father are one,' with that in John 17:21: 'Father, I pray that they all be one just as You, O Father, are in Me and I am in You'; and yet, according to the rule of faith, the Church believes that the Son and the Father are one in a unity of essence."

¶122. We respond. We can look for that rule of faith from nowhere else but from very clear passages of Scripture which prove the deity of the Son of God. Bellarmine says very clearly (Bk. 2, *de concil.*) that, when the Council of Nicaea defined that Christ is consubstantial with the Father, it drew its conclusion from Scripture. However, let us examine the passage in John 10:30. There it will appear obvious that Christ is speaking about the unity of His essence. First, Christ says, v. 28–30: "No one will snatch My sheep from My hand. My Father, who gave them to Me, is greater than all. I and the Father are one." Therefore He is proving the unity of power between Himself and the Father. But now, the power and essence in God are one. [83] Second, Christ says that He is going to give His sheep eternal life. This, however, is appropriate to God alone, who is self-existent. Third, the Jews immediately felt that Christ had said that He was of the same substance with the Father and therefore wanted to stone him as a blasphemer. Augustine (treatise 48 on John) says: "Look, the Jews understood what the Arians did not understand. The Arians became angry because they felt that one could not say: 'I and the

Father are one,' unless where there was an equality of the Father and the Son." Fourth, as we therefore take the unity of believers in John 17:21 to mean the unity of their will and sense (for Acts 4:32 and Rom. 12:16 explain that in this way), so also we take correctly the unity of the Father and the Son in John 10:30 also as a reference to the unity of Their will, but in such a way that it also includes Their unity of essence (because in God the will and essence are one, something which has no place in humans).

We therefore must not extend a comparison beyond what the subject itself allows. Thus, just as we may not conclude from the fact that God commands us to be holy just as He is holy (Lev. 11:44), that we be perfect, just as He Himself is perfect (Mat. 5:28), and that we be merciful as He Himself is merciful; therefore, holiness, perfection, and mercy are also accidents [84] in God, as they also are in us; I say, just we may not draw such a conclusion, so also we may not conclude that the faithful are one just as Father and the Son are one; therefore, that unity of temperament is only in God. That however is not at all so, because the reckoning of dissimilarity is obvious. The will and essence in God are one, and through the unity of Their essence, They want one thing, They can have one will, for the Father and the Son are one.

¶123. Stapleton provides another example by which to prove that a comparison of passages is an uncertain and deceiving means of interpretation. His idea is that, because the Pelagians explained that statement of the apostle, Rom. 5:12: "... in which all have sinned" so that that "in which" signifies "because of which," because we accept it in that way in Psa. 118 and Acts 7; yet, the Church believes according to the rule of faith that that "in which" means the very sin or certainly the person of the sinning Adam.

¶124. Scripture sets forth that very rule of faith. Although we take that expression "ἐφ᾽ ᾧ" in such a way that it signifies the rendering of the cause, for Varinus, Budaeus, and Suidas prove by examples that people use it in that way at times (an explanation which even Dr. Luther follows), that rule therefore offers no support for that Pelagian error, namely: "[Death] passed into all, because all have sinned. Sin therefore is propagated into all." [85] Augustine (Bk. 6, *contra Julian.*, c. 12) rejects that translation "because" because of the faulty twisting of Pelagius and follows a different translation by which he renders the text in this way: "... in whom, that is, in the first human being, all have sinned originally and commonly as in a single lump." Moreover, he refutes Pelagius in the same place on the basis of those very passages of Scripture which Pelagius had produced in favor of his own way of thinking. He also shows on the basis of the circumstances of the passages that that comparison is also faulty, something which he opposes fiercely against Stapleton.

❡125. Finally, Stapleton proves that an examination of sources is an uncertain and weak means in this way: first, because the very sources are not as pure and uncorrupted as they once were; and second, because the Latin translation today is authoritative. We respond. We have spoken about this in its own place, and have asserted [86] the purity of Holy Scriptures as the sources against those light-shunners. We have also shown that the Council of Trent ought not and could not have won over authentic authority for the Vulgate translation. Third, it is uncertain because there are various interpretations of one and the same source. We respond. If it is enough if they not be contrary nor militate against the rule of faith, whether or not one can and should learn from the very sources which version one should approve of especially. Fourth, it is uncertain because heretics today have snatched off insincerely the name "sources" as a place of refuge for their deceit. You see, sometimes they abandon the Vulgate translation and follow the Hebrew text, and sometimes they abandon the source and follow the Latin version. It upsets me that, on the basis of the sources of the truth, the Romans are convicted of their errors with which they are able to prepare from the Latin version some cover-up for their own errors. That's why Albert Ingolstadt used to say that many mysteries of the (papist) faith lie hidden in the ancient letter of the Vulgate edition. (For examples of this see Dr. Chemnitz, part 1, *examen Con. Trid.*, on the versions of Scripture.) You see, if the streams run muddy, who will forbid us from hurrying to the pure water of the spring? If we ever urge the Vulgate translation, [87] we do that for the following reason, namely, to better restrain the papists who are being forced to stand on its authority. Indeed, it became authentic for them in the Council of Trent. If then we shape our arguments according to the real truth, we follow the sources; if we do this according to man, we press the point of the Vulgate translation against the papists.

¶126. These are those war machines, those battering rams, with which the papists attempt to weaken the use of our means of interpretation, but those means stand unshaken. We therefore conclude that Scripture is, first, perfect. That is, it contains all the things which pertain to faith, behavior, worship, and therefore to the receiving of salvation. There is, therefore, no need to take up for it vagrant teachings. Second, it is clear. That is, it uses appropriate, clear, and lucid language in presenting the dogmas of faith so that there is no need for some external light. Indeed, the rest of the teachings receive their light from clearer passages.

Only that interpretation is legitimate which comes from Scripture.

Third and finally, the rule of faith, the comparison of passages, the observation of the antecedents and consequences, the examination of the sources, etc., are not outside of Scripture. This, therefore, is the legitimate interpretation of Scripture which happens from and through Scripture.

[88] ¶127. Thus Ezra and his colleagues were reading the book of the divine law, Neh. 8:9, clearly, "מְפוֹרָשׁ *mephorash*"; and by explaining it they were giving an understanding of the meaning through Scripture, for from the Hebrew Tremellius reads "בַּמִּקְרָא

וַיָבִינוּ *vaijabinu bammikra."* Peter shows (2.1:20) that we must interpret Scripture with the same spirit with which it was first published. But now, the Holy Spirit speaks to us only in and through Scripture. We therefore must interpret Scripture through and from itself. We must not accept a meaning of Scripture which has been introduced from some other source, nor anything which appears to have been an invention of human judgment as the Word of God.

€128. In Mat. 4, Christ checked the devil who was twisting Scripture with the authority of Scripture and teaches us by His own example to refute our adversaries who are distorting Scripture by comparing the very testimonies of Scripture and applying them prudently and correctly. The ancient rabbis said: "In whatever passage of Scripture you find an objection in favor of heretics, you will immediately find a remedy at its side." Indeed, where Scripture speaks quite obscurely [89], it explains itself immediately in the same place and sometimes very richly in other passages. The prophets shed light on the writings of Moses, and in the New Testament the Old becomes clear.

€129. The fathers discuss this subject as follows. Irenaeus, Bk. 2, *adv. haeres.*, c. 47: "If we shall have committed some questions to God, we shall save our faith and will find out for ourselves that all Scripture which God has given us is harmonious. The parables will agree with those subjects which Scripture speaks of clearly, and things which have been said clearly will unfold the parables. Through the many words of Scripture's statements we shall feel within us one harmonious melody which praises God with hymns, etc." Bk. 4, c. 63: "The explanation of Scripture according to Scripture itself is true and without peril." Tertullian, *de vel. Virg.*: "Rise up, O truth itself. Interpret Holy Scripture which custom does not know." Clement of Alexandria, Bk. 7, *stromata*: "Let them confirm again from Scripture each one of those things which they are revealing from Scripture." Origen, homily 7 on Lev.: "It is a good thing to obtain understanding from Holy Scriptures according to their traditions." Homily 25 on Matthew:" [90] Just as every bit of gold outside the temple has not been sanctified, so every meaning which has come from outside Scripture, however wonderful it may appear, is not holy because it is not brought from the sense of Scripture, which habitually has a sanctified meaning." Hilary, Bk. 1, *de Trinit.*: "The best reader is the person who awaits an understanding from the statements rather than introduces them and who refers back to them rather than bringing in new ones, who does not compel that to appear to be contained in the statements which he presumed he had to understand before reading them. Therefore, when the subject concerns God's affairs, let us concede a knowledge of that subject to God, and let us keep His words with pious veneration, for He is a suitable witness of Himself whose understanding is only through Himself."

Augustine (*de doctr. Christ.*) quite often advises us that we must interpret Scripture from itself. Jerome, *apolog. de libris contra Jov.*: "It is the duty of a commentator not to explain what he himself may wish, but that which what he is interpreting senses." Chrysostom, commentary on Genesis, homily 13: "Let us push straight on to the very target of Scripture, which interprets itself. When Holy Scripture wishes to teach us any such thing, [91] it explains itself and does not allow its reader to err." Vigilius, Bk. 2, *contra Eutych.*, in the beginning: "A varied and diverse error comes forth but from a single source of heretical corruption, a very evil turning point for and the origin of evil which of itself has produced opportunities for all wickednesses. That happens when the force of heavenly statements is tempered by the fault of those who understand them poorly and do not grasp their meaning according to its own quality but siphon it away into other subjects according to the judgment and will of the person reading them." Gerson (*quae verity. sint cred.*) asserts the contrary. Master Johannes, *parvi*, no, 14: "Scripture explains its own rules through itself according to its diverse steps." In *de comm. sub utr. spec*: "Holy Scripture, so to speak, is one connected discourse, one part of which confirms, gives light to and explains the other."

❡130. Those fathers said these things in general about the legitimate means for interpreting Scripture. I think that it will be worth our while to deal with them next in particular.

On the rule of faith.

The first was that we must observe the rule of faith which Scripture presents in appropriate and clear words. On the basis of this theorem, I conclude the following consequences. First, the interpretation of Scripture should be literal [92] and appropriate. Second, we must not diverge from the literal, especially in articles of faith, unless Scripture itself reveal and explain an impropriety. Third, there is no dogma of faith which Scripture does not present elsewhere in appropriate and lucid language. Fourth, we must accept the rule of faith wholly and not oppose the parts thereof to each other. Fifth, if we cannot come to the genuine meaning in quite obscure passages, we still must not depart from the rule of faith.

On the various meanings of Scripture.

❡131. That we may explore more correctly and deeply those consequences, we shall use as an hypothesis the various meaning of Scripture. Bellarmine argues about this subject in this way, Bk. 3, *de verb. Dei*, c. 3: "It is the property of Scripture that it has God as its author so that very often it contains two meanings—literal or historical and spiritual or mystic. The literal is that which the words place before it without means. The spiritual is that which is related to another rather than to that which the words signify without means. We gather this division from the apostle (1 Cor. 10[:11]) where he says that all things happened to the Jews as a foreshadow of us. The literal meaning is dual: the one simple, which consists in

[93] the proper significance of the words; the other figurative by which the words are transferred from their natural meaning to an alien one. Of this meaning there are as many kinds as are kinds of figures."

The more recent theologians establish a triple spiritual meaning: allegorical, tropological, and anagogical. They call it allegorical when the words of Scripture signify, in addition to the literal meaning, something in the New Testament which pertains to Christ or the Church. Thus, in Gal. 4, the apostle shows that Abraham, who actually and literally had two wives, a free woman and a maid servant, as well as two sons, Isaac and Ishmael, signified God, the Author of the two covenants and the Father of two people.

They call it tropological when the verbs or actions are related to something to be signified which pertains to behavior, as in Deu. 25: "You will not muzzle the mouth of the ox which tramples out the grain." We take this literally about real oxen. The spiritual significance is that we ought not stand in the way of preachers when they accept food from the people, as the apostle explains in 1 Cor. 9.

They call it anagogical when the words or actions are related to signify eternal life, as those words in Psa. 95:11: "To whom I swore in My wrath, if they will enter into My rest." [94] We take this literally to mean the Promised Land but spiritually, to eternal life, as the apostle explains in Heb. 4.

The papists' way of thinking.

¶132. Bellarmine goes on and adds: "On the basis of these meanings, we find the literal meaning in every statement of both the Old and New Testaments. It is not improbable that we find plural literal meanings in the same sentence. Every spiritual meaning we indeed find in both Testaments, for no one entertains doubts about the Old Testament that it may have an allegorical, tropological, and anagogical meaning. Very many people feel the same things about the New Testament and deservedly. Although these meanings behave in this way, nevertheless we do not find a spiritual meaning in every statement of Scripture, neither in the Old nor in the New Testament. After all, that statement: 'You shall love the Lord, your God' and similar commandments have but a single meaning, that is, the literal. Now that we have established these matters in this way, it befits both us and our adversaries that we seek effective arguments solely from the literal meaning, for that meaning which we collect immediately from the words we are sure is the meaning of the Holy Spirit. On the other hand, [95] the mystic and spiritual meanings differ. Although they may edify when they are not contrary to faith and good behavior, we nevertheless do not always agree whether they are the intent of the Holy Spirit." Bellarmine says all these things in the same words.

Our way of thinking.

❡133. Our thoughts about this subject are as follow. There is one proper and genuine meaning of each passage, and that is the one the Holy Spirit intends. We gather that from the actual genuine meaning of the words, and from this literal sense alone we take effective arguments. Allegories, figures of speech, and anagoges [or allusions] are not different meanings but different conclusions on the basis of a single meaning or various accommodations of that one meaning and subject which the letter expresses. We can apply the same account in different ways so that we treat it allegorically, tropologically, or anagogically. (We are no longer examining whether this division of the mystic sense of the words is sufficiently suitable for expressing those types of the mystic meaning. We would call tropology more correctly "the moral explanation," because "τρόπος" most usually signifies "behavior" [Dionysius, *eccles. hier.*, c. 2; Augustine, *de vera relig.*, c. 50; Jerome, *ad Hedib.*, on Isaiah 1]; and others here and there [96] confuse "anagoges" and "allegories." But if by reason of subject matter, a question rises about the difference between allegory and anagog, why is not also a different class of its spiritual meaning established which deals with the Church Militant, Christ, the Sacraments, etc.?) In the meantime, there remains one proper and literal meaning of the words which describe the account.

Allegory.

❡134. The fathers sometimes look for various allegories, and these very different, from any one account of Scripture; but heaven forbid that we say that there are so many meanings of that one passage that, as Bellarmine says, we cannot agree whether they are the intention of the Holy Spirit but are rather the arbitrary accommodations of a single, literal meaning. Furthermore, when Scripture itself interprets anything figuratively, then the whole and complete meaning of the passage lies not in the words taken literally, but part is in the sign and part in the things signed. Each of these considered separately and of itself contains only part of the meaning; but when we connect both we discover the full and complete meaning. You see, we then reach agreement on the basis of the interpretation of the Holy Spirit Himself that that account contains this figurative meaning about which we are uncertain [97] in the case of the allegories which the fathers have imagined.

❡135. Furthermore, what Bellarmine says, namely, that this is a property of Holy Scripture (because it has God as its author) that it very often contains two meanings, the *Mythologiae* of Fulgentius, Natalis Comes, and Palaephatus about not believing histories, the commentary of Sabinus on *Metamorphosis*, and other writings refute in detail. And what is the connection in the fact that Scripture had God as its author; therefore it has the property of containing two meanings? On the contrary, in fact, because the Creator of the mind and tongue speaks in Scripture, therefore it speaks clearly. That whole thing which the mind embraces Scripture expresses in speech. That is the best discourse which represents fully and clearly the meanings of the mind if we must still comprehend what someone intends for himself in his own words and in what sense we must accept them if someone says anything but conceals something else. Wise people do not approve of this.

¶136. We therefore accept that statement of Bellarmine that we can and should seek effective arguments solely from the literal meaning. If allegories, tropologies, and anagoges were the genuine meanings of Scripture, we surely would seek effective arguments [98] from them as pronouncements of the Holy Spirit. Because Bellarmine denies this (and rightly so), he surely in this way denies that allegories, tropologies, and anagoges are various meanings of Scripture. We approve of that statement of Jerome, on Mat. 13: "We cannot effectively confirm dogmas of faith from mystic meanings," something he repeats in his commentaries on Zac. 8 and on Mal. 1. (See also Augustine, Bk. 2, *de peccat. merit.*, last chapter; *de doctr. Christ.*, c. 9; and epistle 48, *contra Vincent.*) Furthermore, we must understand this as a reference to the mystic meanings which interpreters have invented. After all, if the apostles interpret anything allegorically, we would seek firm arguments from those allegories.

¶137. But come now; let us speak in greater detail about allegories. Augustine (Bk. 15, *de civ. Dei*, c. 27) asserts: "We must not agree with those who accept the history alone without an allegorical meaning nor with those who accept the figures alone and reject the truth of history." Again, Bk. 17, *de civ. Dei*, c. 3: "It seems to me that those are very much in error who opine that no historical accounts in that genus of literature signify anything other than that which happened in that. I think that those are very daring people who contend that there all things are wrapped in allegorical meanings." [99] Jerome (*epistle to Pammach.*) complains most justly about Origen that he allegorizes in such a way that he takes away the truth from history. He says that in their allegories the fathers are quite generous with them, but today some are quite hostile to allegories. What, then, should we decide about allegories?

The difference between allegory and type.

❡138. Those who discuss these subjects carefully advise that there is a difference between allegory and type. It is a type when some deed of the Old Testament is revealed to have foreshown or foreshadowed something which happened or was to happen in the New Testament. It is allegory when something from the Old or New Testament is explained in a new sense and accommodated to a spiritual doctrine or instruction of life. A type consists in a comparison of actions. Allegory is involved not so much in activities as in those discourses from which one picks out useful and hidden teaching. Types are drawn to some specific main points about Christ, the Church, etc., but allegories extend far more broadly and are spread through all sorts of subjects. Consequently, one can explain one and the same account typically and allegorically. If I should say that the account of David and Goliath signified the battle of Christ [100] with the devil, that will be an explanation by type. If I shall have said that it signifies the battle between flesh and the spirit, it will be an allegory. The fathers, however, do not always observe this distinction. The apostle asserts that he is saying the words of Gal. 4:24 through allegory. Literally speaking, however, they are figurative. For this reason, Chrysostom in his commentary correctly advises that Paul used the word "allegory" for "type" here.

How far should we advance in allegories?

❡139. You ask: "How far should we advance in allegories?" We respond. First, we must use special care concerning the literal meaning which we must draw from the words and the very context, for that meaning which we conclude directly from the words we are certain is the meaning of the Holy Spirit. We can draw from that literal meaning different teachings, exhortations, comforts, and refutations of our foes. Basil (*hexaem*) commends very highly this literal explanation of Scripture.

Second, if the Holy Spirit Himself interprets something in

Scripture figuratively or allegorically, there we are safe in following the allegory, for we can be sure that the Holy Spirit looked back to that.

Third, in moral commandments, promises, warnings, [101] and treatises of dogmas we should not look for allegories. Jerome writes, commentary on Gal. 4: "We should not look for allegories in commandments which have to do with life, nor in those matters which are clear and obvious."

Fourth, those interpreters who seek allegories in any passage at all of Scripture are foolish and perverted, according to Augustine (Bk. 8, *de Gen. ad lit.*, c. 1); and those who believe that all things in Scripture are said figuratively are deceived.

Fifth, we can treat the ceremonial laws of the Old Testament figuratively because they were shadows and types of coming blessings.

Sixth, we can deal with histories allegorically but in such a way that the historical truth is preserved without distortion. David defeated Goliath, and thus Christ defeated the devil, and in this way the pious affection of the flesh, etc. In the meantime, however, it remains that David once defeated the giant Goliath.

Seventh, allegories in dogmas do not produce firm proofs. (I make exceptions of those which Scripture itself presents.)

Eighth, therefore, the use of allegories befits discourses which are to be delivered to the people rather than those which are to convince our adversaries of the truth. They please, stir up, and remove boredom when one applies them decently and moderately. For this reason, they are especially suitable for introductions.

[102] Ninth, we must rest upon this assiduously that the allegories be appropriate but especially that they are analogous to faith.

€140. But how must we shape allegories that they be suitable and analogous to faith? The target for all Scripture is Christ.

We therefore must explain as best as possible His office, His blessings, and His kingdom in allegories. It is in this way that Christ accommodates to Himself the manna and the brazen serpent and the accounts of Solomon and Jonah in John 3 and 6 and Mat. 12. It is in this way that the apostle accommodates the type of the Passover lamb, the mercy-seat, the water from the rock, etc. to Christ in 1 Cor. 5, Rom. 2, and 1 Cor. 10. He must have a precise perception of the articles of faith, therefore, from prior and very clear pronouncements of Scripture, if anyone should want to go off to allegories, and he must be very careful that he not bring forth in allegories what is contrary to the analogy of faith, that is, contrary to the steadfast and everlasting way of thinking of Scripture concerning the dogmas of faith. Here there is a slippery slope, and therefore judgment and circumspect prudence are necessary.

¶141. One will gain great favor for an allegory if he can prove its sources from Scripture itself, for one brief word is often the key [103] to open the allegorical meaning. In this way, we can accommodate all the parts of the commandment about the Passover lamb to Christ and His faithful people, because Paul says, 1 Cor. 5:7: "Christ, our Passover, was sacrificed for us." In this way, we can pluck out very aptly and sweetly those allegories which we gather from the words of Scripture, and from those very words of Scripture we can apply some support or certainly some light.

¶142. However, we must be careful not to pursue allegories for too long, for they will be unpolished and harsh, and we must take care that they not conflict with the principal parts of the history which we want to deal with allegorically. It is not just to deal with them overly long. That people may find favor with them, we should touch upon our allegories briefly with subtlety and a sort of sweet austerity. Briefly, therefore, it is not anyone's forte to handle allegories appropriately and fittingly. Those therefore for whom allegories are less exciting should act soberly and prudently here. Those who handle allegories in an untimely way without judgment can easily reach the point that the highly skilled hold them in contempt, the ill-willed deride them, and the weak become offended because of that. [104] The ancients surely faulted Origen under this charge.

When necessity persuades us to use allegories.

❡143. Hyperius warns us very correctly that necessity itself compels us to pursue allegories, but sometimes utility persuades this alone. The necessity of explaining through allegories comes from three causes. The first is when Scripture carries a falsehood ahead of itself, unless you should accept the idea that a trope lies beneath it. Thus, in Psa. 91:13 we read: "You will walk upon the viper and the lizard, and you will trample underfoot the lion and the dragon." We do not read that Christ did this. Therefore we must explain it as a reference to the devil, the world, sin, and death which He overcame and defeated in battle.

This happens, second, when the words of Scripture, taken as they are in their grammatical sense, produce an absurdity. In this way, Scripture attributes human emotions like anger, fury, and ennui to God. Yet these are not in harmony with the spiritual and immutable nature of God. We must explain them, therefore, as a reference to effect and not to affect.

It happens, third, when the grammatical sense conflicts with the rule of faith. Augustine, Bk. 3, *de doctr. Christ.*, c. 10, writes: "Whatever in Holy Writ we cannot relate properly to decency of behavior nor to the reality of faith we must recognize as figurative." In c. 16: "Speech containing a commandment and which seems to demand [105] a disgraceful or criminal act or which seems to avoid usefulness or kindness is figurative." Thus, Christ orders that we pluck out an eye or cut off a hand or foot (Mat. 18:8 and 9); and yet, if we should take this in a literal sense, it militates against the command of the Lord: "You shall not kill." Therefore, as Chrysostom advises, homily 17 on Matthew: "Christ does not speak these words to refer to treating the connection of our body parts with violence but rather to fault an evil of the will. He is not ordering us to mortify the parts of our body but the members of the old Adam which are upon the earth, namely, fornication, uncleanness, lust, corrupt concupiscence, and greed, as Paul explains (Col. 3:5)."

Sometimes utility persuades us.

¶144. Usefulness persuades us to employ allegories when the actual words taken grammatically appear to offer no useful teaching or instruction, or, if some indeed appears but nevertheless comes forth far more richly when we add an allegorical interpretation. Thus we read that, when Laban deceived Jacob by substituting Leah in place of Rachel, because the god of this world deceives many [106] with a love for earthly things so that they think it is Rachel, that is, a most beautiful and lasting blessing; but, when they wake up from the sleep of corrupt concupiscence, they acknowledge that that is Leah.

¶145. Augustine (*de util. cred.*) divides the procedure for explaining Scripture a bit differently, for he claims that it is a four-step process. The first is according to history, namely, when Scripture teaches that something was written or happened which did not happen. The second step is according to etiology, when Scripture shows why something was said or happened. The third is according to analogy by which we have a demonstration of the agreement of the two Testaments. The fourth step is according to allegory, when Scripture teaches that we must not accept literally what was written but must understand that figuratively. This last in his book *de vera relig.*, c. 50, he subdivides into the allegory of history, the allegory of deed, the allegory of speech, and the allegory of Sacrament.

Etiology.

¶146. We have spoken enough about allegorical meaning. Furthermore, that process of interpreting according to etiology is not a new meaning in addition to the literal, but we should certainly relate it thereto. You see, in it we are not departing from the grammatical sense but [107], after explaining the cause for the deed or statement, we are merely rendering it clearer. In quite many passages we cannot examine the true and genuine meaning absent the help of etiology, namely, that we may come to know who says something to whom and for what reason or purpose that comes forth.

Analogy.

Analogy also does not present some new meaning of Scripture but compares the statements or happenings of the New Testament with the statements or happenings of the Old and reveals their harmony. This is just as "every writing which is equipped for [leading] into the kingdom of heaven must be like the head of the household who produces out of his treasury both old and new things" (Mat. 13:52).

Conclusions of the rule of faith.

¶147. Now that we have explained these matters in this way, we return to our conclusions which we have deduced on the basis of that theorem that we must observe especially the rule of faith in our interpretation of Scripture. The first was that the interpretation of Scripture ought to be literal and proper. A confirmation and true understanding of this conclusion can open up from those things which we have just said about the various meanings of Scripture. Irenaeus says, Bk. 2, c. 46: "That meaning is sound and safe which Scripture posits clearly and without ambiguity with those words."

[108] ¶148. The second conclusion was that we must not depart from the literal meaning, especially in articles of faith, unless Scripture itself show and explain an impropriety. This follows from the first conclusion. Had the Holy Spirit wished us to understand something else, He also could have spoken differently. This mean-

ing, therefore, is undoubtedly the meaning of the Holy Spirit which we gather from the very words. If that meaning contains some impropriety in the articles of faith, the actual words explain this elsewhere. Throughout the entire Church, the prophetic and apostolic books are attributed to the Old and New Testaments. The very serious warnings of the Jesuits, however, are well-known, by which they forbid us from departing from the words of the Testaments taken literally. Chrysostom writes, commentary on Isa. 5: "We must sometimes interpret allegorically from some passages of Holy Scripture where it is fitting for us to follow the mind of Scripture and to use in this way the figure of an allegory. After all, we are not permitted to give our hearers authority to accommodate discourses by themselves to whatever matters or persons they wish. Rather, Scripture itself stands ahead and interprets Scripture."

¶149. The third conclusion was that there is no dogma of faith [109] which Scripture does not present elsewhere in appropriate and clear words. This follows from the first conclusion, for if we must reveal and explain an inappropriate meaning of the words in the articles of faith from Scripture itself, surely all the dogmas of faith are explained elsewhere in appropriate and clear language. We confirm this very thing from the perfection and clarity of Scripture; for, if among the articles of faith, we must refer anything which Scripture does not present elsewhere in appropriate and clear language, the perfection and clarity of Scripture surely perish. Statements which Scripture may speak inappropriately can be explained in different ways. Accordingly, those alone which Scripture speaks appropriately and clearly offer a sure and unshakable way of thinking.

Irenaeus writes, Bk. 2, c. 46: "Because parables can accept many explanations of themselves which affirm their search for God, they abandon what is certain, indubitable, and true and really hurl themselves into irrational peril; I say, as a result who will not confess a love of the truth?"

Augustine, epistle 48: "Who is there who will not try very shamelessly to interpret something set in an allegory in favor of himself unless he should have obvious testimonies with which [110] to shed light on obscure matters?" Thomas, part 1, q. 1, art. 10: "Nothing essential to faith is contained under a spiritual meaning which Scripture does not treat clearly elsewhere through the literal meaning."

¶150. The fourth conclusion was that we must accept the whole rule of faith and not oppose parts thereof to each other. The reason for this rule is obvious because all the things which pertain to the rule of faith are the utterances of the Holy Spirit which we cannot and should not oppose to each other. Therefore, wherever Scripture presents an article of faith, we must retain the literal meaning and not oppose it to the rest of the articles of faith. For example, the Arians deny the deity of the Son because there is one God. They are not noticing on the basis of the rule of faith that they must believe in not only the unity of the divine essence, but also the trinity of Persons. The Tritheites introduce three gods because here are three Persons of the deity, but they are not noticing on the basis of the rule of faith that they must believe in not only the trinity of Persons, but also the unity of the divine essence.

¶151. The fifth conclusion was this: although we may not arrive at the genuine meaning in the case of the more obscure passages, nevertheless, we must not depart from the rule of faith. Indeed, we must work assiduously [111] to arrive at the genuine meaning of each passage. If, however, we should be unable to thoroughly examine that, let us be careful lest we introduce anything contrary to the analogy of faith—something we have spoken of earlier.

Augustine says, Bk. 11, *de civ. Dei*, c. 33: "Our treatment of the obscurity of this passage (that we take 'light' to mean the good angels and 'darkness' to mean the evil ones) has not been useless, because, even if we have been unable to determine the intent of the author of this book, we have not strayed from the rule of faith which the faithful have known sufficiently well through other passages of the same authority."

Augustine again, Bk. 1, *de Genes. ad lit.*, c. 21: "When we read the divine books in so great a multitude of true understandings which we pluck from few words, we are also strengthened by the soundness of the catholic faith, something we love very much, for it has sensed that what we are reading appears to be certain. If this certainty is hidden, that surely is something which the circumstance of Scripture does not hinder, and it is in harmony with sound faith. If, on the other hand, we cannot deal with and examine the circumstance of Scripture, this at least is what Scripture prescribes. You see, not to understand what the writer especially meant is one thing; but it is another to stray from the rule of piety. [112] If one should avoid both, the reader receives prefect fruit. If, however, he cannot avoid either, even if the will of the writer be uncertain, to have held onto a way of thinking which is in harmony with sound faith is not a waste of his time."

The example of the words of the Holy Supper clarifies the use of the conclusions.

¶152. The use of these observations and conclusions which we have set forth is very great in the interpretation of Scripture. Let us make the matter clear with an example. Bellarmine, Bk. 3, *de verbo Dei*, c. 9; Stapleton, *relect princ. fidei.*, controv. 6, q. 7, and others, argue in this way:"Because we have debated about the words of the Supper for so many years already, in fact, for so many centuries, and have not yet settled the matter, therefore Scripture cannot say what the true meaning is. The interpretation of Scripture from Scripture itself therefore is doubtful and uncertain. The means of interpretation presented earlier are insufficient. We therefore require some infallible and authoritative judge and interpreter in addition to Scripture itself."

¶153. However, let us follow the lead of these rules. The interpretation of Scripture ought to be proper and literal, especially in the case of articles of faith. But now, those passages which deal with the Lord's Supper present an article of faith. Therefore, we [113] must retain their words in their proper and literal sense. In turn, we are not to depart from the letter in the articles of faith unless Scripture itself explain an impropriety. But now, nowhere does Scripture teach that the words of the Supper need an explanation like this: "The bread is a sign of the body of Christ. The wine is a sign of the blood of Christ." They have not yet been able to provide some suitable example of, as they call it, their own sacramental metonymy. Therefore, we must not introduce into the words of the Supper such metaphoric and figurative language. Furthermore, there is no dogma of faith which Scripture does not present elsewhere in proper and clear words. Scripture, however, treats openly the dogma of the Supper in Mat. 26, Mark 14, Luke 22, and 1 Cor. 10 and 11; and this is the proper *sedes* of this doctrine. Therefore, we must accept those passages in their proper and literal sense.

Whether the rule of faith compels us to abandon the literal meaning.

¶154. They may say that the rule of faith compels us to depart from the literal meaning, namely, because, according to the rule of faith, we must assert that the body of Christ is a true and natural body; and also because Christ ascended into heaven with His own body; I say, if that should happen, the fourth observation helps; that is, that we must accept the rule of faith wholly and not [114] oppose parts thereof to each other. Scripture teaches both that the body of Christ is a truly human body and yet, that body is truly distributed in the Supper. Therefore, we must believe both and not oppose the one to the other. After all, the body of Christ is not only human, but is also the special body of the Son of God. Christ not only ascended into heaven, but He also sits at the right hand of the Father.

¶155. The following statements are not contradictory: "The body of Christ is a true body," and: "We eat the body of Christ in the Holy Supper"; because in both instances the words of Scripture teach in the proper and literal sense thereof. We must not hear Scripture in only the one, namely, that Christ has a true body, but also in the other: that this true body is present in the Supper. If they absolutely wish to deny the one or the other, namely, either the reality of His body or its eating in the Supper, they should explain to us the reason why they wish to deny the eating of the body of Christ in the Supper on the basis of the reality of His body rather than the reality of His body on the basis of its asserted eating in the Supper. If they should say that the reality of His body is an article of faith, we must ask them from what source they know this. They [115] will certainly respond: "From Scripture and indeed from its literal meaning." I say, however, that Scripture also teaches and in the literal sense that the body of Christ is present in the Supper and that the people eat it there. Therefore, that presence and eating of Christ's body in the Supper is an article of faith.

The objection of the Marcionites.

¶156. Some Marcionite may say that the body of Christ is not a true and natural body because we distribute it in the Holy Supper for the people to eat. We, therefore, must take those passages which claim that the body of Christ is a truly human body are in a figurative sense so that its wholeness stands together with the article about the Supper. This surely cannot happen otherwise than we say, for we must assert and believe both, namely, that the body of Christ is truly human and yet it is eaten in the Supper, and that we must not oppose these articles to each other but accept both with the obedience of a simple faith. Unless he hold that as firmly fixed, even a Marcionite will depart from the literal meaning of those passages with the same license by which he abandons the literal meaning of the words of the Supper which assert the reality of the human nature in Christ.

[116] **The objection of Bellarmine.**

¶157. Bellarmine concludes too broadly (Bk. 3, *de sacr. Euch.*, c. 19) that if we take the words of the Supper literally, we must introduce transubstantiation. He says: "The bread is changed either metaphorically or truly and really." We respond that a third possibility is also given, namely, that the bread is changed sacramentally. That is, it becomes a medium, a vehicle, and instrument through, in, and with which we distribute the body of Christ. Also, the word "this" in Christ's words indeed denotes the true bread but not alone (for what would the construction of "ἄρτος τουτο" be?), but the entire context, for when two things are united in some way, it is the usual custom that the predicate expresses the more dignified and less obvious in sense, but not the other part obvious in meaning.

Whether the literal meaning in the Supper conflicts with the ascension of Christ.

¶158. Because we have begun to deal with the controversy over the interpretation of the words of the Supper instead of using an example, the very size of the subject demands that we discuss them in greater detail. Perkins argues in his book *de unic. ratione conc.*, p. 49, that the preservation of the literal meaning in the words of the Supper conflicts with the Ascension of Christ and with the nature of the Sacrament; but, contrary to that new meaning that the bread is a symbol of the absent body of Christ (That's the way he writes!), it is in harmony with the analogy of faith. "First, Christ truly ascended into heaven; that is, He was carried up from earth locally and visibly. We therefore are not going to take His body with our mouth in the Supper, but we perceive it in heaven by faith. Second, He was born of the Virgin Mary. He therefore had a real and natural body. As a result, we agree that the bread in the Supper cannot literally be His body but can only be a symbol thereof."

¶159. We respond. The bread is His body not in essence but sacramentally so that, at the same time that we eat that mystic body, we eat the body of Christ. This does not conflict with the analogy of faith, as we have just shown. No necessity therefore compels us to forsake the literal meaning and seek a new meaning. We are not asking whether Christ ascended into heaven with His real body or whether He has a real body, but whether the fact that we claim that His body is in the Supper conflicts with the article of His Ascension and with the reality of the body of Christ. We shall say more about this later.

[118] Whether it conflicts with the circumstances of the given passage.

¶160. Second (as Perkins says), "the literal meaning conflicts with the circumstances of the given passage. First: 'He took,' and: 'He broke.' Here it is not likely that Christ, sitting as He was in the midst of the disciples, took into His own hands His body and broke it. The bread, therefore, is only a sign and seal." We respond. "What God has joined together no man should separate." The evangelists relate that Christ not only took the bread and broke it, but that He also blessed it. It was that blessed bread that He distributed. He also added clearly what He was distributing when He declared that it was His body. It is not true nor is it likely that Christ distributed mere bread to His disciples; otherwise, He would have been playing tricks on them with His deceitful words.

Second: Perkins says, "'...which is handed over for you.' By no means can one say that bread was handed over for us, but we can say that His body was given up for us. The bread, therefore, according to the letter is not His body but is symbolic thereof." We respond. We invert this. In the Supper, Christ distributed that which He gave up into death for us. But He did not give up for us mere bread, but He gave up His own body into death for us. He therefore distributed not bare bread, but His body.

Third, "'The cup is the new covenant' is not something taken literally but by metonymy [119]. Nothing therefore keeps it from being metonymy in like manner in these words: 'This is My body.'" We respond. Paul says that the cup is not simply "the new covenant" but he adds: "…in the blood of Christ," that is, because of the blood of Christ, of which it is the "communion" (1 Cor. 10:16). Matthew and Mark speak in this way: "This is My blood of the new covenant," which coupling confirms the literal interpretation. The cup does not *signify* the new covenant but *is* the new covenant. How? Not of and in itself but in the blood of Christ which He is revealing to those who are drinking it.

Fourth, "Christ Himself ate the bread, but not His body." We respond. What Scripture, however, asserts is this: that He shared in the mystic bread along with the disciples?

Fifth, "'Do this in remembrance of Me.' Christ, therefore, is not physically present to His mouth, but He is present spiritually to the faith of the heart." We respond. He is confusing the substantials of the Supper with its salutary fruit. Christ instituted the Supper in commemoration of Himself. He said: "Do this in remembrance of Me." Is Christ therefore absent from the Supper? Certainly not, because the Supper was instituted in remembrance of Christ. He therefore was actually present there when He distributed His body.

[120] Sixth, "'…until He come.' Christ therefore is absent from His body." We respond. He departed, and here He is. He will return, and He has not deserted us. We are waiting for Christ's return from heaven, and nevertheless, we believe that the officiant is distributing Christ's body in the Supper, for He commands us in His word to believe both.

Seventh, "Christ did not say: '…under the appearance of the bread' or 'in the bread,' but 'this,' that is: 'this bread is My body.'" We respond. The hypothesis is false, because the particle "this" denotes the bread alone.

❈161. Third, he says that the literal sense conflicts with the nature of the Sacraments in which we must posit an analogy between the sign and the thing signed, which cannot exist if the bread literally is the body of Christ. We respond. We must pass judgment on any Sacrament at all on the basis of its description in its proper *sedes* nor must we pretend that there are general unwritten pronouncements about the Sacraments of both Testaments. Furthermore, what keeps us from positing an analogy between the bread and the body of Christ, even if the former is actually present on earth?

Whether the new meaning is in harmony with similar passages.

¶162. Fourth, Perkins says that the new meaning is in harmony with similar passages of Scripture like Gen. 17:10: "This is My covenant between you and Me… You shall circumcise the flesh of your foreskin… that it be a sign of the covenant." [121] We respond. He is proceeding from the particular. Here "covenant" is posited for "a sign of the covenant." In the Supper, therefore, "body" is used for sign of the body. Furthermore, when God says that circumcision is a covenant, He is describing circumcision according to its form, and thus we have: "Circumcision is a covenant," that is, a Sacrament and a covenantal act, just as Baptism is also a covenant. However, when He says that circumcision is a sign of the covenant, He is describing the Sacrament of circumcision on the basis of its purpose, just as Paul says in Rom. 4: "Circumcision is a seal of the righteousness of faith," clearly and effectively sealing it. Therefore, as Augustine says, *confess.*, art. 13: "The Sacraments are the signs and testimonies of the divine will."

Second, 1 Cor. 10:4: "They were drinking from the spiritual Rock, and that Rock was Christ." We respond. The apostle is speaking about that spiritual Rock which was accompanying the Israelites, but this did not signify Christ but actually was Christ Himself. From this spiritual Rock everyone was drinking but with this distinction, namely, that the wicked were drinking only in type [figuratively], but the godly were drinking in type and by faith simultaneously.

Third, Rom. 4:11: "He received the sign of circumcision which sealed the righteousness of his faith." We respond. The apostle clearly explains the word "sign" in this way, [122] that we take it to mean the sealing seal.

Fourth, Exo. 12:11: "It [the lamb] is the Passover"; and shortly after (13:9), we read that the lamb was the sign of the Passover. We read neither [literally] in Moses, much less does an explanation of the nocturnal prayer-leader have a place. Even if we were to concede that circumcision signified a covenant in a special way, nevertheless this did not allow the distinction between the Sacraments of the Old and New Testaments to be applied to the matter of the Supper. Rather, in the case of the former, they were properly shadows and figures, but in the case of the latter, the actual likeness and substance of the thing foreshadowed have a place.

Fifth, Acts 22:16 indicates that Baptism is the washing away of sins. We take the word "Baptism" to mean the whole Sacrament, not just the external washing but also the addition to the element the words of regeneration, adoption, and eternal life. By this reckoning, Baptism does not signify the washing away of sins but absolutely truly the washing of regeneration. Where, however, does Scripture say that the washing of water in Baptism signifies the washing away of sins? We shall speak about this in greater detail later.

Sixth, John 6:35: "I am the bread of life." We respond. Christ is the bread of life, for we take the word "bread" not metonymically but [123] metaphorically. If there is such a sacramental metonymy in the words of Christ, what will the paraphrase thereof be? Obviously this: "Christ signifies the bread of life." He, however, does not *signify* the bread of life but most truly *is* the bread of life which can satisfy our spiritual hunger.

Seventh, 1 Cor. 10:16: "The cup of blessing which we bless—is it not the communion of the blood of Christ? And the bread which we break—is it not the communion of the body of Christ," that is, a sign of communion? We respond. What is this license for imagining that "communion" means a sign of communion? Where then finally does Scripture speak clearly and lucidly about the Supper? What will the paraphrase of "The bread is the communion of the body of Christ" be? That is: "The bread is the sign of the communion of the sign of the body." You see, they want the word "body" in the words of the Supper to have to be taken in such a way that it is a sign of the body, and thus the body will be the sign of the sign. On the contrary, in fact, from this apostolic passage we can take a very firm argument in favor of our way of thinking that the mystic bread is not a signification of the body of the absent Christ but, rather, a present communion.

[124] **Whether the new meaning is in harmony with the precepts of logic.**

¶163. Fifth, that new meaning is in harmony with the precepts of logic, for a disparate thing is not said about a disparate thing, except through tropology. We respond. This false hypothesis recurs that the word "this" denotes the bread alone. Furthermore, there is no trope in these propositions: "God is a human" and "A human is God," is there? We must look not for what befits the precepts of logic, but for what agrees with the words of Christ. Justin says: "The case violates the Word."

Whether the new meaning is in harmony with the accepted manner of speaking.

Finally, Perkins says that this new meaning is in harmony with the accepted manner of speaking. Thus, we say "fasces" for "imperial power"; "scepter" for "kingdom"; "toga" for "peace." We respond: What writer ever speaks in this way: "The fasces are imperial power, the scepter is the kingdom, a toga is peace?"

¶164. After this digression which that writer wanted to

establish in the actual matter of this problem regarding the interpretation of Scripture, let us return to our established plan. We said that we must accept the full rule of faith and not oppose the parts thereof to each other. Indeed, the articles of faith accepted in their proper and literal sense are not inconsistent with each other. Human reason, however, imagines for itself contradictions, [125] and this is the source of all heresies. Tertullian, *advers. Prax.*, c. 18: "Scripture is not endangered that you must run to its aid with regard to your proof so that Scripture may not appear to contradict itself. It has a rationale when it claims that there is one God and when it reveals that the Father and the Son are two Persons. That is enough for it."

Human reason in the articles of faith.

⁋165. Human reason has no license to pass judgment about a true contradiction in the articles of faith. Otherwise, it would be established as the schoolmaster of Scripture, for its rule is not suitable for understanding thoroughly either divine power or divine will; not the former, because "no one has ever seen God. The Son, who is in the bosom of the Father, has told us" (John 1:18); and not the latter because "God can accomplish superabundantly beyond our understanding" (Eph. 3:20); "We must take captive every thought under obedience to Christ" (2 Cor. 10:5); and: "We must beware that philosophy not ravage us." (Col. 2:8).

The use of philosophy in sacred matters.

⁋166. Here a misstep is likely. Therefore it will not be beside the point if we speak in some detail about the use of philosophy in the interpretation of Scripture. It can have three uses: organic, constructive, and destructive.

1. The organic use.

We use it organically if [126] our reason brings along with it the grammatical properties of the words, the dialectic observance of order, the explanation of rhetorical figures, and the physical understanding of natural phenomena which it has drawn from the philosophic disciplines to pluck the treasure of divine wisdom concealed in Scripture. We recommend this use very highly. In fact, we say that it is necessary. To this use, we must relate those quite honorific praises thereof which the ancients attributed to philosophy and especially to logic. (See Augustine, Bk. 1, *contra Crescon.*, c. 15, v. 20; Bk. 2, *de doctr. Christ.*, c. 31; and *contra Academ.* c. 13; Basil, commentary on Isa. 5, etc.)

2. *The constructive use.*

¶167. As far as the constructive use of human reason is concerned, we must hold the following. There is a sort of natural knowledge of God (Rom. 1:19–20), but we must hold that subordinate to that wisdom which the divine Word has revealed. If it disagrees, human reason must yield to the Word. In those matters where reason agrees, it receives strength and certainty therefrom. Briefly, as a maid and servant to a lady, reason serves her mistress and reverently rises in her presence. Gerson, Bk. 1, *de consol. theol*, prop. 1, writes: "Theology [127] does not reject philosophy. We rather take the latter into obedience to the former." To this belongs also the allegory of Philo in his book *de cherub.*, which compares philosophy to Hagar but theology to Sarah.

¶168. Scaliger argues (*exerc.*, 6, sect. 3) that a master receives from a master questions, declarations, statements, and conclusions in two ways. One is when the understanding of an inferior thing depends wholly on the principles of a superior one, something which happens in the case of subordinate sciences. The other way is when a master admits from what another has posited what he even knows without that, but not as principles of his own nor as proved by the other, as if he himself were unable to prove that, but that he may examine and pass judgment on that. In the latter way, the theologian receives some points from the philosopher. The theologian receives from the philosopher that theorem: "God exists." However, he does not receive that as if he could not know that from Scripture as the natural principle of his own wisdom, absent the principles of philosophy, but because he knows the truth of that in his examination thereof, according to the norm of his own principle.

Gerson, Bk. 3, *de consol. Theol.*, prop. 4, writes: " If theology approves the teachings of Philosophy as true, if it accepts them as correct, if it accepts them as salutary; it uses them [128] by its own right and makes them universal. If they are quite obscure, it sheds light on them; if they are mixed with errors, it separates the precious from the cheap, keeps the former, and casts away the other."

3. The destructive use.

⁋169. That the destructive or critical use be legitimate, it ought to be arranged in this way. First, we must refute erroneous teachings from the foundations of Holy Writ as the one proper principle of theology. Later, we can add philosophic reasons to show that the false dogma resists not only the light of grace but also the light of nature. However, when we have proved the truth of some dogma firmly from the unshakeable foundations of Holy Scripture, we must allow no philosophic reasons, however specious they may appear, to lead us away from it.

Statements of antiquity regarding this subject.

⁋170. To this are pertinent the godly statements of antiquity. Justin says, q. 117: "It cannot happen that an assertion of those things which divine power has created beyond nature be added by natural reason." Tertullian, *de praescript.*: "What does this have to do with Athens and Jerusalem? What is this to the academy and to the Church? – or with heretics and Christians? Our project concerns the porch of Solomon." Chrysostom, homily 5, on 1 Corinthians: [129] "To wish to comprehend divine matters from philosophy is to handle glowing iron not with tongs but with the fingers." The same, homily 21, on Genesis: "It is a very dangerous thing to entrust matters of faith to human reasons."

Ambrose, commentary on Psa. 118: "Have no dealings with philosophy lest its drag our faith away from the truth through the elements of this world." We know that the Arians fell into faithlessness when they thought that they must draw conclusions of the generation of Christ from the usage of the world. They abandoned the apostle, they have followed Aristotle." Bk. 2, *de fide.*, c. 5: "Remove his arguments when questions of faith arise." Bernard, epistle 190: "What greater thing is there contrary to faith than to be unwilling to believe, for you cannot handle it with reason? We praise Mary because she went beyond reason by faith. Zechariah was punished for he tested his faith with reason."

Junilius, Bk. 2, *quaest.*,c. 30: "Faith understands those things which reason teaches. When reason fails, faith surpasses it." Ansh.[12], letter concerning faith to Pope Urban, c. 2: "If anyone can understand, let him thank God. If he cannot, let him not raise up his horns to brandish them against Him, but let him lower his head to worship Him."[13]

From this, Altisiodorus, *praefat. summae*: "The argument in Aristotle [130] is reason which creates faith in a doubtful matter, but in Christ the argument is faith which is creating reason."

With reference to this way of thinking of the philosophers.

⁋171. What do the philosophers admit about this way of knowing? Plato (*Timaeus*) says: "To what extent we must confirm something to the philosopher about divine matters, to that extent we must confirm that very matter by the divine utterances." In his *Phaedrus*, he says: "Two vehicles of true reasons lead people back from errors to knowledge, one of which is through the proof of

---

12 The reference is uncertain.
13 I cannot render this pun in English: "*Non immittat cornua ad ventilandum, sed submittat caput ad venerandum.*"

known things." This manner of knowing he calls 'ἀπόδειξιν - demonstration.' The other is truth which descends divinely to us, and this he names 'θεῖον λόγον - the word of God.' In the same place, he concludes that human wisdom isn't going to do anything beyond those things which we have from the oracles. He also says, as Theophrastus relates, *Aeneas Gazaeus*, p. 720: "In the works of Philo he said that we must believe him so far until someone wiser than he appear, but no one is wiser than God."

Aristotle somewhere makes an exception of "very patient words" (which some people take to mean "divine authority"), and because of them does not disapprove of suspending agreement. In his *metaph.*, he praises that trite statement of Simonides: [131] "In divine matters and those which surpass nature we must believe God alone." In Bk. 1, *anal.*, c. 7, conc. 59, he requires that the relationship of terms in a proof not become "a transition into another genus, a force from this genus to a middle or lofty one."

The Arab Alphraganus (Bk. 1, *protrep.*) wanted divine matters credible to true faith to be of a quite lofty level from the comprehension of which human reasons become crippled. As Peter Gregory relates, *comm. art. mirab*, c. 1, p. 1: "People cannot reach those divine matters." Scaliger says neatly, *exerc.*, no. 365, sect. 3: "We should not judge the things which surpass the laws of nature on the basis of the laws of nature." *Exerc.*, no. 365, sect. 3: "All the worse, some of those theologians have persuaded themselves that the limitless fields of our religion can be measured with the ten-foot pole of the ancients." Sect. 9: "It is also of concern to our godliness and to the immensity of God to sense the things which we cannot sense, and indeed to sense in and through Him the things which we cannot sense by ourselves." Erasmus produces a very beautiful example in his *symb. catech.*, 2, p. 43: "If some ignorant person should raise a ruckus against such a philosopher as was Aristotle or Pythagoras, or someone who was more learned than both about the first matter, about the principles of things, [132] about infinity and the different size, movement, and force of the heavenly bodies, and if that person should go on about all subjects which one cannot know, won't he hear that he is arrogant and insane? How much greater than insanity, then, is it not to believe divine philosophy, much of which the human intellect does not attain? Certainly, however great the difference of learning there is between God and man, it is greater in its infinite parts than between the wisest human and the most foolish country bumpkin."

The confession of the Calvinists.

❡172. The force of the truth has earned the assent of those who we complain are not observing this very thing everywhere. Calvin, Bk. 3, *instit.*, c. 32, sect. 4: "It is unworthy that we reduce the works of God to this law that so that we dare disapprove of the idea that a reckoning of them does not at the same time stand firm for us." Beza, *epigr.*, p. 249: "With what word did God relate to us the things that humanity cannot know with its own reason?" Sadeel, preface to his *opera theol.*, *de meth. disp. theol.*: "Because theology stands above all fields of knowledge, to subject it to the principles of philosophy is not only inappropriate but also very wicked and unworthy." Aretes, part 1, prob. 2: "What is that impudence [133] to subject the divine mysteries to the common laws of nature. Because those mysteries are inexplicable to all human reason, we are to worship them rather than rail at them."

Zanchius, Bk. 5, *de natura Dei*, c. 2, p. 620: "The Word of God and human prudence are always waging war with each other." Peter Martyr, Class 2, *loci commun.*, c. 1, ❡25: "First, Holy Writ ought to reveal that which we want to believe. Next, if we cannot achieve this, let us rely upon our faith and set reason aside." Mornaeus, preface to his book *de vera relig.*: "Heaven forbid that human reason become the measure of our faith so that it cannot even exist because of the ignorance and corruption of nature." The same, preface to his book *de Euchar.*, p. 44: "Thomas is correct in restricting his teaching to Scripture, which is abhorrent to those who want to dispute on the basis of the principles of philosophy and other disciplines against that rule of logic: 'Do not cross over into another genus'; that is: 'Do not pass over from one science to another.' After all, according to the true use of logic, our rationalizing should deduce from the principles of one field of knowledge theorems pertinent to the same from these corollaries." They are absolutely correct in saying these things.

[134] **Whether something is true in philosophy which is false in theology.**

❡173. "Therefore," you ask, "is there anything in philosophy which is false in theology?" We respond. We have spoken about this matter in some metaphysical disposition about what is true. From it we shall transcribe the things which are pertinent to this. The same thing cannot be true and false at the same time, for there is no entity which exists and does not exist simultaneously. Nevertheless, people say some things which are true philosophically but false theologically. We must understand this in a certain respect, namely, by reason of a faulty application a virgin gives birth, and a virgin does not give birth. These are not contradictory of themselves, for we understand the latter naturally according to the ordinary course of nature. Physics, after all, speaks about those things which happen naturally and ordinarily; therefore we must accept them as its axioms with this limitation. We understand the former to happen through the supernatural and extraordinary power of God. If someone then should wish to oppose the former to the latter, he is opposing this axiom, for it is a non-philosophy to accept a particular and subordinate as a simple universal. We must oppose nothing which is natural to the supernatural, for nature is not opposed to its Creator.

[135] "God is the Lord of nature; nature is His servant.
How correct it is to follow the awesome laws of the Lord."

The use of a thing does not extend itself more broadly than the thing itself, but philosophic principles are natural.

❡174. Those, however, act in an inverse and perverse order who attack the literal meaning in some article of faith on the basis of philosophic principles. In the articles of faith, we must not desert the literal sense because of an absurdity of reason.

Corrupt and regenerated reason.

Grynaeus (*disp. Heidelb. de* coena, theses 25 and 26) and Bucanus (locus 48, p. 711) distinguish between corrupt reason and that which became spiritual after regeneration. To the former, they are relating those things which Scripture says about taking the intellect captive under obedience to Christ, about being careful of the theft of philosophy, etc. However, they say that we should not take away trust in the latter, for it becomes spiritual after regeneration. What should we decide about this subject?

❡175. We respond. We can and should understand human reason correctly and in two ways: in one way, in its riches which it has acquired through using its own talents and principles such as are common notions, feelings, experience, and induction; in the other, in those things which it has received into its own bosom from a different source, namely, [136] from divine revelation. On the other hand, we can and should understand it in one way as it has been left and released to itself; and the other, as it has been enclosed and corrected within the sphere of the divine word. Or third, as it runs about unrestricted by its own principles wherever its feet carry it, and the other as it runs about under rein, checked through the Word of God and restricted under obedience to Christ. Or fourth, in one way such as it is in a human and in a philosopher, and in the other such as it is in a Christian human or Christian philosopher, not insofar as he is a human and philosopher but as he is a Christian person and a Christian philosopher. This is just as Dr. Schröder sets forth these points very skillfully in *de princ. fid.*, sect. 2, ❡3.

Whether the reborn person who attacks the literal meaning does this according to his reborn reason.

¶176. Now then, the question is this: When a person already reborn attacks the literal meaning in the case of the articles of faith on the basis of the principles of reason, must we say that he is doing that according to his regenerate reason? We respond. Absolutely not! After all, even if the reason of such a person has been reborn; to the extent that he is willing to debate against the articles of faith, to that extent his reason is no longer reborn, for the reborn reason argues on the basis of the principles of the Word. [137] He who argues against the mysteries of faith from the principles of reason does not do this insofar as he is a Christian but as a person who is abusing philosophy. Therefore, he is not committing this sin as a person who was born of God (1 John 3:9), namely, insofar as he is such a person and to the extent that he has received the grace of regeneration. If, however, he should wish to follow the lusts of the flesh, he sins and becomes subject to death (Rom. 8:13). The reborn reason, therefore, is not opposed to the articles of faith, namely, to the extent that it is reborn and to the extent that it follows the lead of the Word. If, however, it wishes to attack the Word of God on the basis of its own principles, it sins and is no longer reborn.

An example.

¶177. Let us make the subject clear with the example which we also applied earlier. The question is this: Is the body of Christ truly, really, and substantially present in the Supper? Our churches affirm this because Christ says: "Take. Eat. This is My body." However, our adversaries deny this on the basis of this principle: that a true and natural body cannot at one and the same time be in more than one place. They add that reborn reason cannot claim otherwise about a body; and, therefore, we must listen to its reason. However, I say that reborn reason (to the extent that it is such) makes its claims about the articles of faith [138] on the basis of the Word of God and does not go beyond the limits thereof. But now, the Word of God says: "This is," "Take," "Eat," "This is My body." If reason argues against these words of Christ on the basis of its own principles, it is no longer regenerate, but is following its own lead. We should listen to it no more than we should listen to a philosopher arguing against the resurrection of bodies according to that principle: "No undivided body which has once perished can return the same in number." Nor should we listen to it anymore than we should listen to an anti-Trinitarian arguing against the mystery of the Trinity on the basis of this principle: "One thing cannot be three things"; or to an Arian arguing against the eternal generation of the Son on the basis of this principle: "A thing once born comes after the begetter."

The objection.

⟪178. "But," you say, "when reason debates against the presence of the body of Christ in the Supper, it is not simply resting upon its own principles but also on the declaration of Scripture concerning the reality of the body of Christ." We respond. Reason should listen to Scripture not only in the one matter, namely, that Christ has a true body, but also in the other, to wit, that the true body of Christ is present in the Supper. We must accept the rule of faith in its entirety. The question here [139] is not whether the body of Christ is a true body but whether, while the reality of His body stands firm, we may infer correctly therefrom that God cannot cause that true body to be present in the Supper. They say: "The nature of a body does not allow this, for it is finite." But from what source do they know for a fact that it is contrary to the body of Christ that it be present in plural places at the same time? Certainly from the principles of reason, for Scripture says the opposite. The final resolution of the argument, therefore, returns to the declaration deduced from the principle of reason, and that principle opposed in a faulty way to the words of Christ. Therefore, let us remove that sophisticated "hidey-hole" which they want to prepare for themselves in that distinction between reborn reason or—as they speak, "spiritual reason"—and unregenerate reason.

The observation of Basil.

¶179. There is that observation of this locus which St. Basil sets forth in some letter. (Let us not conclude rashly that what was written was not written by him.) Indeed, Nazianzen says correctly (Bk. 5, *de theol.*) that the things which have been concluded from Holy Scripture accordingly must be considered as if they had been written therein. Here there is instead a need for great caution, for human reason often behaves very stealthily and accommodates Scripture to its own inventions according to its own will. [140] Let this then be our rule: We must claim that whatever we conclude from Scripture which is opposed to other clear passages of Scripture has not been a legitimate conclusion.

Concerning the reconciling of passages.

¶180. Let these be the things we have said about the rule of faith, indeed, in quite great detail, but the subject itself kept requiring this. We shall speak more briefly about the rest of our points. We have said earlier that lack of clarity in some passages of Scripture stems from the fact that they appear to be in conflict with other passages. You see, although there has never been a true contradiction in Holy Scripture, according to Chrysostom (homily on Genesis) because "all (that sacred writing) is God-breathed; nevertheless, an apparent contrariety and contradiction occasionally offers itself." Augustine, Bk. 5, *de Genes. ad lit.*, c. 8: "We must try to cause that no absurdity nor contrariety which may offend the way of thinking of a reader be considered to exist in Holy Scripture." Origen, commentary on Rom. 3: "The person who gathers faithfully and fully the meaning of the sacred books ought to show that the things which appear to be contrary in Holy Scripture are not contrary."

¶181. To reconcile that apparent contrariety we must apply the following remedy, [141] namely, that we seek the true and genuine meaning of each passage from the very words and circumstances thereof. Because a contradiction has no place in Scripture; as soon as we agree about the genuine meaning of each passage, therefore, we have removed every contrariety which used to appear to be therein. Augustine wrote, Bk. 3, *de doctr. Christ.*, c. 2, and Bk., 1, *de Gen. ad lit.*, last chapter: "We must remove the ambiguity and conflict which appear in Holy Writ on the basis of the consequences and circumstances of the very text."

The general rule.

¶182. Let this be the rule of reconciling apparent contradictions: If some contrariety seem to crop up when we have compared some passages among themselves, let us teach that the opposition is not of the same subject but only of the name, or not in some certain respect and not according to or in the same way, or not at the same time. Thus, in Mat. 10:10, Christ forbids the apostles to take a bag or two tunics or sandals or a staff for the journey. What He says in Mark 6:8 appears to be contrary to this: "And He commanded them that they take nothing along for the journey except only a staff but no wallet, no bread, no money in their purse but to wear sandals." The reconciliation is this: [142] In Matthew, we understand "staff" to mean that which arms a person as a weapon; in Mark, we take it to mean a walking stick, which assists travelers. "Sandals" in Matthew are new shoes which the shoemaker makes carefully for traveling. In Mark, "sandals" are not new, but those which the feet wear daily. We can also say that we should take the words of Christ in Mark comparatively, for even if they are equipped with neither a staff nor shoes, which nevertheless appear especially necessary for travel, the disciples ought not be hindered in their purpose.

Special rules with respect to circumstances.

¶183. To this general rule, we can add as many special rules as we need, and these we can distribute into special classes by reason of their circumstances. These are the circumstances: person (which speaks, to whom one speaks, about whom one speaks, before whom one speaks); the occasion for the speaking (as advice, purpose, time, place, and manner).

Person. To the circumstance of purpose pertain the following rules. First, persons in Scripture often have two names, according to Jerome, *adv. Helv.* Thus Gideon is called "Jerubbaal" (Jud. 6:21), and "Jerubbesheth" (2 Sam. 11:21). Abimelech (1 Sam.21:3) is called "Abiathar" in Mark 2:26. Thus Solomon (1 Sam. 12:24) [143] is called "Jedediah" in v. 25. Thus Simon is called "Peter" and "Cephas." Second, different persons often are one-named. Examples occur in the genealogy of Christ which Mathew and Luke describe. Third, sonship is either natural or legal. Natural is by birth; legal, by adoption. Thus, in writing the genealogy of Christ, Luke uses the natural order; but Matthew, the legal. Fourth, different statements are made about the reborn because they have within them two people, so to speak: the old person and the new one. Thus, Paul says that the reborn are "sold under sin" (Rom. 7:14), namely, by reason of the old person. The reborn commit no sin (1 John 3:9), namely, by reason of the new person. Fifth, Scripture says some things about Christ according to His divine nature, and some things according to His human nature, etc.

¶185. *Of advice, purpose, and occasion.* To the circumstance of advice, purpose, and occasion pertains the following rule: "We must take our understanding of statements from the causes of speaking them." Thus, Christ (Mat. 19:21) presents to the young man who belonged to the school of Pharisees and who was boasting falsely about his perfect fulfillment of the Law this special commandment, namely, that he sell all [144] he had and distribute the proceeds to the poor and in this way follow Christ. Christ clearly wanted to convict the fellow for not fulfilling the First Commandment concerning loving God above all things. In this way, Christ presents the Gospel to the terrified and contrite, but He sends the scribe who had become swollen by the opinion of his own merits back to the Law (Luke 10:26).

¶186. ***Third, the circumstance of time.*** We can teach many rules about the circumstance of time, for that old rule is true: "Distinguish the times and you will bring Scriptures into harmony." First, some statements speak about Christ's state of exinanition, and some about His exaltation. Second, we take the time as complete or incomplete. Third, its parts are taken either conclusively or inconclusively. Thus, we have in Mat. 17:1: "After six days Jesus took Peter, etc." But in Luke 9:28 we have: "It happened about eight days after these words, etc." Matthew posits exclusively only the intervening days, which flowed along inclusively. Luke also counts the extreme days inclusively. Fourth, in a more complete numbering, often what is lacking or which remains is not counted, as Augustine notes (q. 47, on Exodus). Thus, in Jud. 11:26, we read that the Jews lived in Heshbon and Aroer for three hundred years, although a precise computation nevertheless would provide more. [145] So also we hear commonly that there were seventy Greek translators, although there were seventy-two. Fifth, sometimes a finite number is stated for an infinite one: "The just person falls seven times," (Pro. 24:16) "I shall sing Your praises seven times a day," (Psa. 119:164) etc. Sixth, in sacred computing, because of the wickedness of the ruler, his name or the number of years during which he served poorly are omitted. In 1 Sam. 13:1, we read that Saul ruled over Israel for two years. Here read between the lines "legitimately" or, as Lyra says, "according to law." Seventh, if a king has been hindered by external warfare, old age, or illness and while still alive has established his son as his successor, in the computing of the years of the father and the son ruling together, the years are counted sometimes together and sometimes separately. They used this rule in counting the years of the kings of the Israelites. Eighth, what we read in Mark 15:25: "It was the third hour when they crucified Jesus," and in John 19:14. It was the sixth hour, and then [Pilate] said to the Jews: 'Behold your king.'"; I say, these statements people reconcile in different ways. Some acknowledge a fault of the Greek writer, who wrote "ζ" instead of "γ."

Some people make a distinction between a beginning and a completion. Augustine says that [146] the Jews crucified Christ with their tongues in the third hour; and the soldiers killed Him with their hands in the sixth hour.

Furthermore, this seems to be a very simple reconciliation that the Orientals distinguished the artificial day in different ways, both in twelve equal hours commonly called "planetary hours," and also into quadrants (as the night into four watches), which are named from the hour immediately preceding each.

¶187. *The circumstance of place.* The following rules deal with the circumstance of place. First, the sacred writers often attribute two names to one place. Second, they often attribute one name to different places. Thus, "Jerusalem," "Jebus," and "Salem" denote one city. "Cana" was the name of two places; "Succoth," of three places. The first was in Egypt (Exo. 12:37); the second, in the tribe of Gad (Jos. 13:37); and the third, in the tribe of Manasseh (1 Kin. 7:46). Third, they often name a place with that name which people used at that time when they lived and wrote. Thus, in Gen. 12:8: "After leaving there he went forth to the mountain toward the eastern area of Bethel." That place was so-called at the time of Moses, but at the time of Abraham it was called not "Bethel" but "Luz" (Gen. 28:19), etc.

¶188. *The circumstance of manner.* With reference to the circumstance of manner we can hand down [147] many rules. First, some are said individually; some, distributively. Second, some are said simply; some, comparatively. We are to honor our parents; but in certain respect, we must hold them in hatred (Luke 14:26). That is, we must put aside their authority, namely, if they command something which is contrary to the heavenly Father. Third, special statements diminish general ones, just as the Jesuits say: "In all legal right, genus is diminished through species." Fourth, moral laws are placed ahead of ceremonial laws. Fifth, the Second Table of the Law yields to the First. Sixth, some statements speak about the nature of a thing *per se*; but some statements we understand through their accidents. Thus Christ says that He came not to send peace but the sword (Luke 12:51), namely, because Satan and the wicked stir up persecutions against the teaching of Christ. Up to this point, we have been speaking about the rule we must observe in reconciling apparent contradictions. Many of these rules the faithful and diligent interpreter of Scripture will conclude. As far as we are concerned, this is enough to have revealed the sources.

⁋189. We advise one more thing yet about the reconciliation of passages, namely, that it is the best procedure for reconciling if we can give an arbiter, so to speak, from Scripture; to wit, some third passage of Scripture [148] which harmonizes with those conflicting ones, or which confirms a reconciliation which we have produced. Thus, the reborn have been sold under sin (Rom. 7:14); and the reborn person does not commit sin (1 John 3:9). How are we to reconcile these? The apostle responds, Rom. 7:22–23: "I take delight in the Law of God according to my inner person, but I see another law in my members which is battling against the law of my mind and making me prisoner of the law of sin which is in my members." In this way, the teachings of the Law and Gospel appear to be contraries, but the apostle is establishing himself as their judge, Rom. 3:31: "We are not destroying the Law through faith, are we? Heaven forbid! We are rather stabilizing the Law." Gal. 3:21: "The Law is not contrary to the promises of God, is it? Heaven forbid." In this way, they appear to be contradictory. "We must observe circumcision" (Gen. 17:14). Acts 15:24: "We must not observe circumcision." Christ established Himself as the arbiter, Mat. 11:13: "The Law and the prophets all the way to John."

On the removal of an obscurity which has developed; first, on the basis of subjects.

¶190. If any passages of Scripture taken of themselves and singly are obscure, they are obscure either because of their subjects or because of their words. To remove an obscurity produced from their subjects, in addition to the illumination of the Holy Spirit which we must obtain with serious prayers [149], it is useful to hold on to some specific axioms in any article of Christian doctrine which are like pole-stars and norms toward which we must drive the treatment of the rest. We can say that such axioms are catechetical or elementary. Commonly we call them "theological rules," but the industrious and faithful interpreter of Scripture can gather them according to the series of theological commonplaces. We shall lead off with an example here.

¶191. In the article "On God," we must observe the following axioms. "The external works of the Trinity are indivisible, although the order and difference of the Persons has been preserved" (Augustine, epistle 99; Bk. 1, de Trinit., c. 5; and here and there elsewhere). Athanasius, orat. contra greg. Sabell., etc.: "The essential attributes are common to the three Persons of the Trinity. There is nothing in God which is not God Himself." Bernard, Bk. 5, de consid. ad Eugen.: "That which works is one essence common to the three." Nazianzen, orat.2, de theol. opera: "The works which God does outside every creature and within Himself are not common to the three Persons, but are only of one Person. An exclusive prayer used about one Person of the Trinity does not exclude the others." Cyril [150]: "God is one and unmixed, and trine indivisibly. In divine matters, let us not divide His substance nor mix up the Persons." "No sooner do I consider the One than I receive an illumination of the Three. No sooner do I distinguish the Three than I am brought back to the One" (Nazianzen, de S. Bapt.).

¶192. In the article "On Christ," the following axioms are

presented. First, "the properties of His nature become common to the Person" (Vigilius, Bk. 3, *contra Eutych.*, and Theodoret, dial. 3). "In Christ there is one thing after another but not one Person after another" (John of Damascus, Bk. 3, *de orth fide*, c. 5). "In the works of the Mediator, both natures act along with the communication of the other" (Council of Chalcedon). "Whatever things are said to have been given to Christ in time we understand to have been given according to His humanity" (Athanasius and the ancients here and there).

¶193. In the article "On the Law," these are the axioms. Whatever accuses and condemns sin belongs to the Law, whether that occurs in the Old or in the New Testament. The forensic and ceremonial laws in the New Testament have been abrogated. The moral law was not first published on Sinai but was engraved in the hearts of people before the Fall. The reborn are not under the curse of the Law; but in the meantime, they are not free from obedience. The moral laws [151] signify all sins of the same kind, their causes, occasions, incentives, and opposed virtues under sin as that is defined name by name. The rule and measure of obedience are affirmative in the commandments: "You shall love God with all your heart"; and in the negative: "You shall not covet." God commands not only the hand and all the body parts, but also the whole person. The promises and threats which have been added to the Law must be understood along with a condition; the former, with the condition of perfect obedience; the latter, with the condition of repentance. The promises of this life which God has given to the godly we must understand with the exception of the cross.

¶194. In the commonplace "On the Church," the axioms are as follows: "Because good people are mixed with evil in the Church Militant, as a result something is often declared about the whole Church because of its more noble part. Here the Jebusite dwells with the Jerusalemites. Here, in the garden of the Head of the household, are the stink-weed and the silver fir, the bull-nettle and the myrtle. In the flock of Jacob are black animals and white ones, lambs and kids; in Peter's net, good and bad fish; in the Lord's field, lilies among the thorns; on the threshing floor of the Lord, grain and chaff; in the cellar of Christ, wine [152] along with vinegar, oil along with the dregs thereof," as Chrysostom speaks. "Holy Scripture sometimes speaks in the role of the Head of the Church, namely, Christ, and sometimes in the role of the body" (Augustine, on Psa. 40). "Outside the Church there is no salvation. He does not have God as his Father in heaven who does not have the Church as his mother on earth" (Augustine, Bk. 4, *de symb.*, c. 10).

At times Scripture unites them and joins these together closely: God, the Word, Father, the Church, salvation, eternal life, etc. We can gather more in these very commonplaces as well as in other passages of Christian doctrine. Here it is enough to have pointed our finger at the sources.

Second, from the words and phraseology.

☾195. That obscurity which stems from the words and phraseology of Scripture can receive relief from the grammatical explanation of the words, from the observation of the common idiom of the original language, and from a rhetorical explanation of tropes and figures. Therefore, the faithful interpreter must know the languages in which the Old and New Testaments were written. (In our disputation concerning Scripture, we spoke about this subject.) Therefore it is advantageous to gather some rules according to specific classes which explain the common idiomatic Hebrew language. We again start with an example.

[153] ☾196. We know how the grammarians distribute the parts of speech. We must collect the rules of these according to their order. The following are the rules for nouns. Scripture frequently take proper names for patronymics and people of the same clan, as Ishmael and Esau; and Jacob and Israel for all posterity.

The name of a truly special accident is posited for the actual thing, like "dry" for "earth"; "desirables" for "treasures." A noun is often placed for an adverb: "Just righteousness," that is, "justly." "Death is swallowed up in victory"; that is, it is destroyed victoriously. Abstract nouns are often used for persons. Thus "foreskin" is used for Gentiles; "circumcision," for Jews, etc.

¶ 197. The following are the rules concerning verbs. Among the Hebrews verbs of knowing often connote a feeling of the heart. "The Lord *knows* the way of the upright"; that is, "He approves, He promotes." The Hebrews use neutral verbs of the Third Conjugation transitively. "God 'arises' the sun"; that is, He causes it to rise. "He triumphs us in Christ"; that is, He causes us to triumph. Simple verbs are often used instead of compounds, as "to call" instead of "to call upon." They often take verbs in an habitual sense. Thus "to sin" indicates not only the action but at times also the habit [to sin repeatedly]. [154]

With reference to participles, we supply these rules. Often participles are posited for nouns. Thus "πηράζων - tempting" is used for "tempter." The present participle is used instead of the present indicative: "glorying" instead of "we glorify."

The rules for adverbs are these. Adverbs are often used instead of nouns as "the day tomorrow," that is, "tomorrow." The adverb "*donec* - until" indicates the duration of existence of something so that in the meantime it hints that it later ceased to exist or that the contrary occurred. It befits us to gather more such rules. (Regarding this subject, see Flacius, part 2, *clavis*, treatise 3, and Abdias Praetorius, *de phras. Script.*) We must also observe idioms not only as they are placed absolutely in parts of a speech but also in terms of rules. But let someone who is skilled in languages rise up and show us something absolute in this area. Here it is enough to show the sources.

¶ 198. We must explain things said tropically or figuratively on the basis of rhetorical rules. Furthermore, Scripture has some peculiar figures, about which see Flacius, part 2, *clavis*, treatise 4. [155] We call it "anthropopathy" when an author attributes human parts and emotions to God. We can gather rules according to specific classes with which we can explain the tropes and figures which writers used in Scripture. Synecdoche is very common in Scripture. Through it a general word signifies something special and vice versa: "nothing" for "very little"; "no one" for "a few"; "eternal" for "for a long time." Augustine (Bk. 6, *contra Jul.*, c. 12) writes: "Here observe the restrictions which we must demonstrate from Scripture itself in the articles of faith." Thus when we read: "Christ suffered for all," it is not enough to say: "The universal word 'all' is taken for 'many'; and therefore it is taken in this way in this passage." On the contrary, we must show that in this very matter it is taken restrictively. Earlier, we said that in the articles of faith we must not abandon the property of the words unless Scripture itself reveal and explain the impropriety.

"Enallege" of the past tense in place of the future is frequent in the utterances of the prophets because of the certainty of the matter foretold. "Ellipsis" signifies either the brevity or the swiftness of the emotions. "Pleonasm" signifies either force or emphasis or multitude or distribution or [156] diversity and variety. Here let someone stand up who may also show us something absolute. Here it is enough to show the sources.

Parables and likenesses.

¶199. Regarding parables and likenesses (which are nothing other than continued metaphors) we must observe that the same thing may be able to supply likenesses on the good side or on the bad side. Thus "yeast" is taken positively when Christ says: "The kingdom of heaven is like yeast"; but, on the contrary, negatively when He says: "Be careful of the yeast of the Pharisees." Also, in parables all parts cannot be accommodated always nor simply to the proposed argument. Rather, we must observe carefully what can square or head in a direct line at the present target especially well through analogy. (See Chrysostom, on Mat. 20.) In the case of parables, we must not press the point of individual words or parts beyond and outside of what has been established and to what they are applied in Scripture; nor should we construct other dogmas therefrom which differ from what Scripture demonstrates in taking them up.

Furthermore, a knowledge of subjects causes figurative and parabolic statements to become clearer when people perceive the natures of living beings [157] or stones or plants. (See Lemnius, *de herbis Bibl.* and *de feriis Bibl.*)

The comparison of passages.

⟨200. A comparison of passages provides much help to come to a thorough knowledge of the force of words and phrases and thus to a true understanding of Scripture. By such a comparison, passages are set next to each other as parallels so that their meaning shines forth more clearly. In Acts 9:22, "Saul became stronger and confounded the Jews who were dwelling at Damascus by proving with testimonies which he put together (the way workmen who intend to put something together are in the habit of fitting individual parts together with each other that each may square precisely with the others) that He was the Christ."

⟨201. The fathers commend this comparison of passages. Origen (on Mat. 13) writes: "When we compare things to comparable things which have some likeness of discourse which says the same thing both in the meanings and in the dogmas, as: in the mouth of two, three, or even more witnesses who have been cited from Scripture every Word of God is founded and confirmed." Homily 24 on Numbers: "What we seek in Scripture we find more easily if we bring forth from several passages matters which were written about the same subject."

[158] ⟨202. Here that precept is pertinent, namely, that the plainer passages explain the more obscure; and the more explain

the fewer. Irenaeus, Bk. 2, c. 47: "Parables are in harmony with those passages which speak clearly, and those which are obvious unlock the parables." Tertullian: "We must understand the fewer passages according to the more; and one discourse should not subvert many others, and we shall have to take that one according to all rather than against all." Basil, *ascet.*, Rule 267: "Doubtful things which are said in an obscure way are perceived in the passages of inspired Scripture on the basis of the concordant things which are articulated plainly in other passages." Augustine, Bk. 2, *de doctr. Christ.*, c. 9: "For shedding light on obscure statements let us take examples from the more obvious ones, and let some testimonies of certain statements take away doubt about uncertain ones." Augustine again, Bk. 3, *de doctr. Christ*, c. 26: "Where statements are posited quite clearly, there we must learn in what way we must understand them in obscure passages." Jerome, commentary on Isa. 19: "We have the custom of connecting the clear passages of Scripture with the obscure ones and to proclaim with clear language what Scripture said earlier in puzzles."

¶203. **1. *The comparison of a given passage with itself elsewhere.*** The comparison of passages is dual. The first is the comparison of a given passage with itself elsewhere. [159] For example, the passage Isa. 6:10 ("Cause the heart of this people to become fat.") is repeated six times in the New Testament: Mat. 13:14, Mark 4:12, Luke 8:10, John 12:20, Acts 28:27, and Rom. 11:8. Moreover, repeated passages sometimes have variations but for the sake of exegesis and brevity. For instance, Psa. 110:1: "Sit at My right hand until I shall have placed Your enemies beneath Your footstool"; and 1 Cor. 15:25: "Christ must rule until He shall have placed all His enemies beneath His footstool." Too: Deu. 6:13: "You will respect the Lord your God and serve Him"; and Mat. 4:10: "You will worship the Lord your God and serve Him alone." Again, Isa. 29:13: "Their reverence toward Me [was taught] by the command of men"; and

Mat. 15:9: "They worship Me in vain as they teach as doctrines the commandments of men." The *parall.* of Junius helps in the comparison of passages like these. Observe also this rule which Dr. Chemnitz sets forth, Bk. 2, *harmon.*, c. 17: "When the New Testament cites from passages of the Old, consider not only those words which are cited, but examine the entire passage that you may consider that part more carefully."

¶204. To this pertain in some way [160] the comparisons of a type with its antitype and of predictions with their fulfillment. Here are some examples. Jonah 1:17: "The Lord had prepared a great fish to swallow Jonah, and Jonah was in the belly of that fish for three days and three nights"; and Mat. 12:39: "A wicked and adulterous nation seeks a sign, but I shall not give one to it except the sign of the prophet Jonah." Psa. 69:22: "They gave me gall for food, and in My thirst they gave me vinegar to drink"; and John 19:28–29: "That Scripture might be fulfilled, He said: 'I thirst.' And there they placed a vessel which was filled with vinegar." Exo. 12.46: "A bone of it will not be broken"; and John 19:36: "These things happened that Scripture might be fulfilled: 'A bone of His will not be broken.'" The person who will observe these points correctly will be "a scribe learned for the kingdom of heaven bringing forth straightway from his treasure both old and new things" (Mat. 13:52).

¶205. 2. *The comparison of a given passage with others.* The second comparison is that of a given passage with others which are either similar or dissimilar. Similar passages are those which are congruent either in phrasing or in meaning. An example of ones which are congruent in phrasing is this: Gen. 3:15: "The seed of the woman will bruise the serpent's head."; and Rom. 16:15: "God will trample Satan beneath your feet." For the examination of such passages, there are concordances of Hebrew, Greek, Latin, and [161] German words extant in all these languages.

¶206. There are far more passages which agree in meaning,

for Holy Writ quite often repeats one and the same subject and one and the same main point of heavenly teaching clearly and consistently. For instance, Deu. 6:4: "Hear, O Israel, the Lord your God is One"; and 1 Cor. 8:6: "Although there are those who are called lords, for you, your God is One." The following works are helpful in examining these: the *thesaurus* of Vogel, the *syntagma* of Judex and the *pandect* of Brunfels. Rather, let someone stand up to deal with each and every one of the articles of faith in such a way that each and every passage of Scripture which treats one and the same subject be placed under some one heading and let him explain any contradiction on the basis of the very words and foundations of Scripture.

¶207. Dissimilar passages are those which are not congruent in phrasing or meaning. It is helpful not only to compare those passages of Scripture which use the same word in the same sense, but also to compare such which use the same word and phrase in a different way. If some passages seem to disagree in meaning, a prudent reconciliation which is in harmony with the analogy of faith may be applied. [162] Any intelligent people are forced to confess that Chemnitz, that great artist in the comparison of passages, is almost peerless.

¶208. **3. Obscurity stemming from the entire context.** Up to this point, we have been dealing with the obscurity which the words or phrases of Scripture reconcile. If any obscurity rises from the entire context and manner of speaking, one will remove that with an observation of the target, circumstances, connection of the parts, and manner of speaking used by any writer. This, you see, is "examining Scripture" (Acts 17:11); "paying attention to reading" (1 Tim. 4:13); "meditating on the law of the Lord" (Psa. 1:2); "searching Scripture" (John 5:39), etc.

¶209. Let us listen to the precepts of the fathers concerning this subject. Clement of Alexandria, Bk. 7, *stomata*: "It is mark of heretics that they deal with Scripture neither as mysteries nor as the body and guide for mining the ore of prophecy." Augustine, Bk. 83, *qq.*, no. 39: "The circumstance of Scripture generally sheds light on the meaning when people deal in careful discussion with those things which are round about Scripture." Augustine again, *de verb. Dom.*, sermon 2: "Let a person read the inferior and superior passages, and he will find the meaning which the corrupt person wanted him to interpret poorly." [163] Hilary, Bk. 9, *de Trinit*: "We expect an understanding of Scripture's statements from their antecedents and consequences." Cyril, Bk. 8, *theses.*, c. 2: "Above all, when we want to understand a passage of Scripture correctly, we must consider three things diligently: the time when what is written was written, the person who speaks it or through whom he says it or about what the speaker said it, and the subject because of which or about which the writer wrote it." Chrysostom, on Psa. 2: "As a building is weak without a foundation, so Scripture is useless unless one finds its target." Lactantius, Bk. 4, *div. instit.*, c. 5: "He who is eager to comprehend the truth not only must direct his heart to understanding the words of the prophets but also must examine very carefully the times through which each of those lived."

❡210. The scope of all Scripture is Christ. We must have a special concern that we find Him in Scripture. The apostle judged that he knew "nothing other than Christ and Him crucified" (1 Cor. 2:2). "All the prophets applied their testimonies to Him" (Acts 10:43). "Moses, the prophets, and the psalms wrote about Him" (Luke 24:44). The Savior says, John 5:39: "Search the Scriptures, [164] for in them you think you have eternal life, and they are they which testify of Me." Just as miners seek out carefully the veins of silver and gold, so we must search that vein of Life, Christ, in Scriptures. Augustine, treatise 9 on John: "Ancient Scripture has no taste, if we do not understand Christ in it." On Psa. 71: "All things which are written in Holy Writ are related to Christ." You, quite appropriately, will relate to the prophetic and apostolic writings what Prudentius says about the ancient Christians: "They speak all things about Christ and through Christ."

❰211. The target of this passage and chief point will become clear from a careful examination thereof. The apostle says about those who would mislead, 1 Tim. 1:7: "They pay no attention about what subject they are speaking, nor do they affirm or deny anything about it." He therefore wants us to hold onto and observe the nature of propositions, what their subject or predicate is, the definitions of individual things, and all the raw materials and arguments of either a writer's full writings or even of their individual parts.

❰212. Of this passage there is that observation that there is, so to speak, a specific and proper *sedes* of each dogma [165] somewhere, but elsewhere Scripture only touches upon that. Moreover, we must pass judgment about any dogma from its proper *sedes* and not from those passages which treat it superficially and in passing. On the contrary, we must urge its treatment as its appropriate *sedes* deals with it. For example, Paul handles the doctrine of justification openly and, as in its proper *sedes*, in Rom. 3 and 4, Eph. 2, and Gal. 2 and 3. The rest of the passages of Scripture which deal with justification we must remand to those chapters. The proper *sedes* of the article on the Supper are Mat. 26, Mark 14, Luke 22 and 1 Cor. 10 and 11. We must draw the doctrine of the Supper from those chapters and not from other passages.

❰213. We could discuss here in general the style of the sacred writings, too, and also in particular the historical, dogmatic, and prophetic books of the Old Testament and the evangelic and apostolic books of the New; specifically, what the diversity of style in all these is; what is special and characteristic in each of them, but we are panting to reach the end. (You can see more about this subject in Augustine, Bk. 4, *de doctr. Christ.*; Junilius, *de partibus sacr. lit.*; Pagninus, *isagog. ad Biblia*; Flacius, part 2, *clavis*, treatise 5; and here and there elsewhere.)

[166] *The aforementioned means of interpretation require three things: 1. prayer; 2. meditation.*

¶214. Let this be enough to have said these things about the means of interpretation. That these may be effective, salutary, and fruitful, three things are required: prayer, meditation and proving.[14] All of these the royal psalmist deals with throughout Psa. 119. We spoke earlier about prayer. We take the word "meditation" to mean the frequent and assiduous study of Scripture which we undertake with an ardent fervor of spirit. "Blessed is he who meditates on the Law of the Lord day and night" (Psa. 1:3). Here the verb *"hagah,"* which Reuchlin says on the basis of Rabbi Joseph, is metaphoric, is taken from birds which make muttering sounds and which thus has two meanings: first, to meditate diligently; second, to discuss endlessly. "Timothy knew Holy Scripture from infancy" (2 Tim. 3:15); and yet, the apostle commanded him to pay attention to his reading (1 Tim. 4:13). After all, the frequent reading of Holy Writ produces an understanding thereof. (See Theophilus, *commentary on Romans.*)

¶215. We therefore must avoid that precocious conceit of wisdom by which the smatterers, when they have once read something in Scripture and have touched those very clear (but deep) springs of Israel like the dog drinking from the Nile,[15] quickly promise themselves that they have an absolutely perfect knowledge thereof in every detail. [167] Dr. Luther often thunders against this conceit of wisdom and says: "In reading Scripture, you will never be too diligent. What you have read diligently, you will never understand too accurately. What you have understood well you will never teach others too faithfully; and what you have taught faithfully, you will never express too zealously with the example of your life."

¶216. To this heading of meditation belongs also this precept: that we consult other interpreters, especially those venerable

---

14 *tentatio.*
15 *canis e Nilo.* An allusion from Erasmus and a fable about a dog and a crocodile.

grey heads of the very early teachers of the Church. Although their interpretations are not authoritative nor to be equated with canonic Scripture; nevertheless we should acknowledge and proclaim their godly labors gratefully. 2 The. 1:19–21: "Do not quench the Spirit. Don't despise the prophets. Test all things and hold onto what is good." We should not judge that God preserved the testimonies of our more godly antiquity in vain but that they might be a sort of aid for examining the meaning of Scripture and that the minds of the godly might be strengthened once they have perceived the true meaning from Scripture. [168]

¶217. Pertinent to this are the words which Augustine wrote, *contra duas epist. Pelag.*, Bk. 4, c. 8: "Although Christ's Church, both Eastern and Western, shuddered at the profane novelties of the Pelagians, I consider that it is pertinent to our concern not only to use holy and canonic Scripture as witnesses against them, something we have already done sufficiently, but also to produce some proofs from the writings of the saints who earlier treated Scripture with their very distinguished reputation and immense glory. This we do not because we are equating the authority of any disputant with the canonic books, so that this is not a case as if sensing something as better or more true by one Catholic than by some other one, but that people may receive a warning who think that they are saying something, just as the Catholic teachers who followed the divine utterances spoke before the empty talk of those men about these subjects, and also that they may know that we are defending the correct and long-established Catholic faith [169] against the recent destructive presumption of the Pelagian heretics."

Let us also look at the example of Jerome, who wrote about himself in a letter to Miner: "It is my judgment to read the ancients, to prove their individual writings, to keep what is good and to not deviate from the faith of Luther." Jerome again, commentary on Gen. 2, p. 27: "It is fitting that we honor the labors of the ancient, for they were great men, but yet they were human beings who could have slipped and who did slip."

3. Proving.

⟨218. With the word "proving" we mean "practice," which Epiphanius (Bk. 2, Vol. 1, heresy 61, p. 221) calls in the Greek "perception." He says: "All the utterances of God are not in need of allegory, but they stand as they read. However, they do need philosophic speculation and perception to see the force of each discourse." But, if we connect "perception" to "contemplation," the consequence will be what Augustine says, *de scala Parad.*, c. 2: "Reading inquires, meditation discovers; prayer demands; contemplation tastes; and for this reason, the Lord says: 'Ask, and you will find; knock, and it will be opened to you.' Seek by reading, and you will find by meditating; knock by praying, and it will be opened to you by contemplating. Reading, so to speak, puts solid food in your mouth. Meditation chews and breaks it. Prayer acquires the flavor. Contemplation is that sweetness [170] which delights and refreshes. Reading is in the bark; meditation, in the pith; prayer, in the demand for one's desire; contemplation, in pleasure of obtaining the sweetness."

Bernard, *de modo orandi*, col. 1252: "Reading first occurs as a foundation. Once the subject matter has been given, reading sends us to meditation. Meditation, however, quite diligently inquires what we should strive after eagerly and, so to speak, digs up, finds, and discloses the treasure; but, because we are unable to obtain that of itself, it sends us to prayer. With all its power, prayer lifts itself up to the Lord and obtains the desirable treasure, which is the sweetness of contemplation. When it arrives, it repays the labor of the aforementioned three, for then it inebriates the thirsting soul with the sweetness of heavenly dew."

⟨219. For the sake of teaching, we claim that this proving or practice or perception is twofold: one in the exercises of repentance, faith, prayer, and godliness so that all these things are earnest and proceed from the inner person; the other, in the cross and distresses (which the apostle calls "fears," [2 Cor. 7:5] and which we commonly call "spiritual testings") both interior as well as exterior. [171] Unless this dual practice and inner tastes, so to speak, of Scripture come, the treatment thereof will be empty and barren.

❡220. The psalmist says, Psa. 119:71: "O Lord, it is good that You have afflicted me that I may learn Your precepts." Isaiah says, 28:19: "Vexation gives understanding." The best path to divine understanding is the school of the cross and calamity. The school of the cross is the school of light.

❡221. It is not our intention to hang the divinity of the divine Word on the dignity or quality of its minister (for we know that "it doesn't matter whether the water to irrigate garden plots passes through a concrete or a silver channel" [Augustine, treatise 5, on John]. Haymo, homily for Pentecost: "Regardless of the inner character of the minister, the Holy Spirit is the interior worker."). Meanwhile, that it be useful to the minister himself and more fruitful for his hearers, we require most deservedly that the treatment of Scripture be that practice and inner taste of divine sweetness, as Psa. 34:9 speaks.

❡222. "If you want me to weep, you yourself must first grieve," says Horace, *de art. poet.* So also, if you wish [172] to set me on fire, you must first be burning. Wood which has the capacity to burn does not flame up unless one moves fire to it, and the person who wants to call up godly feelings in others must himself first have those feelings. The emotions which must descend into the hearts of others must ascend from the heart, and those things which the inner person brings forth also strike the ears of the inner person. Bernard says, sermon to the brothers on the mount: "You will never enter into the meaning of Paul without first drinking in the spirit of Paul."

❡223. Savonarola says, Bk. 3, *de scient. divis.*, p. 800: "If someone consider carefully, he will perceive that he learns Scripture with purity of heart, good works, contemplation, and the illumination of the Holy Spirit rather than with the power of his talents." Gerson therefore draws the correct conclusion (prosa 4, *de consol. theol.*, Bk. 4) that "theology (the mere knowledge of theology), absent the mixing in of faith, hope, and charity, inflates and hinders a person. Cicero describes an orator as 'a good man, skilled in speaking.' Thus, we call a 'theologian' a good man who is learned in the sacred writings not only in the erudition of his intellect alone, but much more in his temperament, so that those things which he understands through theology he transfers through endless pondering into a disposition of his heart and the performance of work. [173] (These are still the words of Gerson.) For just as reason, which is the most outstanding gift of humans, in the case of the wicked, turns into the destruction of themselves and others; so also wine, the better it is, the more raging it causes those to become who do not use it soberly. This happens not by fault of the wine but of those who drink it. We must say the same thing about theology."

❡224. Christ says, John 7:17: "If anyone may have wished to do the will of My Father, he will know about My teaching, whether it be from God or whether I am speaking of Myself." Again He says, John 5:44: "How can you believe, you who receive honor from each other and yet do not seek the glory which is from God Himself?" We read in Wisdom 1:4: "Wisdom does not enter an ill-willed soul, nor does it dwell in the body which is subject to sins." Scripture says several times: "The fear of the Lord is the beginning of wisdom." Think precisely what these statements want for you; and you will find that you will hold onto the subjects of the Christian religion far better if you were to rest more upon the cultivation of the inner person. (We spoke about this in the preface to *meditat. sacrar*; and we perhaps shall say more in its own place.)

[174] ❡225. Note what that martyr of Christ, Ignatius, wrote, second letter to the Ephesians, p. 63: "It is better to be silent

and to live than to speak and not live. The kingdom of God is not in word but in power. It is a good thing to teach, if the one who is speaking practice [what he teaches]. For if one practice what he teaches, he will be great in the kingdom. Our Lord and our God, Jesus Christ, the Son of the living God, was foremost in practicing and teaching these things." Justin Martyr, *paraen.*: "The matters of our religion consist not in words but in deeds."

These have been the lamps of the very early church when people still had a greater respect for conscience than factual knowledge and for heart rather than mouth.

❡226. *The purging of souls.* For the sake of the soul, one could relate to this what the philosophers teach about the purging of souls which is necessary for an understanding of divine matters.

Trismegistus[16], on the first discourse of Pimander, was asked under what agreement someone could ascend to life. He responded: "This could happen when a person who has become a thinker pays attention to his mind, for a mind is not present in all people but only in those who are godly, good, pure, religious, and holy and who yield their body to death, who feel disgust at the enticements of their senses, [175] who prune off the fatal pandering of their senses, lock the door to their shameful flatteries, extinguish the tinder of their lusts; and who, on the other hand, remove themselves far from cowardly, envious, wicked, ignorant murderers and godless people and dwell very far from them."

16 Gerhard's citation of 'Hermes Trismegistus' is intriguing, and may represent a lingering influence (at this point) of Johann Arndt, who was heavily influenced by such sources. A work by Nicolaus Hunnius (one of Gerhard's contemporaries) entitled *Principia Theologiae Fanaticae* (1619), would mark the clear confessional Lutheran denunciation of such occult sources. Hunnius' work has been published in an English translation with the title, *Principia Theologiae Fanaticae (1619): The Principles of the Fanatic Theology* (Repristination Press, 2015). For an analysis of the influence of Hermeticism on Renaissance and Reformation era thought, see James D. Heiser, *Prisci Theologi and the Hermetic Reformation in the Fifteenth Century* (Repristination Press, 2011).

Trismegistus again, seventh discourse of Pimander: "It is especially necessary to remove the clothing which you are carrying around yourself, namely, the cloak of ignorance, the foundation of depravity, the chain of corruption, the dark veil, living death, the sensual body, the tricking tomb and, finally, the familiar thief who hates when he flatters and envies when he hates. He is like a hostile parasol. He carries you off downward to himself lest you perhaps catch sight of the beauty of the truth and of a nearby blessing the corrupting of which you hate, and not at some time sense his snares which he plots against you assiduously. This weakens and blunts the keenness of your inner senses, strangles it with its dense matter, inebriates it with its hateful and disgusting pleasure that you may never hear nor perceive those things which rightly you should hear and especially examine."

Trismegistus a third time, on Part 2 of the first discourse of Pimander: "If you not have made yourself equal to God, you will never understand God; [176] for one knows a similar thing only from something [or someone] similar to himself." *Ibid.*: "One must strip the soul of its body not through a true separation but through the mortification of the sensual pleasures that he may be able to understand divine matters. Too, that he may be changed into God, the soul must receive deification; that is, it must be returned to God as similar to Him as possible." *Ibid.*: "Extend yourself into a size without limit; come out from your body; exceed all time; and let eternity be present. In this way, you will ultimately get to know God."

⁋227. The rest of the philosophers have imitated this philosophy of Trismegistus.[17] Zoroaster writes, *orac.*: "In some way, a person gathers God into himself when he retains nothing mortal

---

17 Beginning with Marsilio Ficino (1433–1499), it was commonly believed within certain circles of Renaissance thought that Hermes Trismegistus was a contemporary of Moses and the first in a succession of pagan philosopher/theologians. (See James D. Heiser, *Prisci Theologi and the Hermetic Reformation in the Fifteenth Century* [Repristination Press, 2011]).

and yet his whole person becomes inebriated with the divine matters which he has drained." *Ibid*.: "Because there are two principal diseases of the soul, to wit, ignorance and ill will or wickedness, the soul also requires two steadfast curers or physicians, namely, instruction and purity of life." He says that they must get into some vehicle that the soul may return to the same place from which it came. Moreover, this vehicle is nothing other than the elevating of the mind into God.

Pythagoras says: "No one should dare speak about God without a light." There is extant [177] a letter of the Pythagorean Lysis to Hipparchus about the purging which must precede philosophy. In it, he teaches that all faults must be driven out of souls that someone may obtain the true knowledge of human and divine subjects. Plato (*sophist*.) says that this purging is nothing other than casting out of the soul that which is corrupt but saving the rest. In his *theatit.*, he teaches that one must escape from the world into heaven that he who is very similar to God may get away. This flight, he says, is the actual likeness of God, insofar as that is within us. Moreover, that likeness exists that we may be prudent, holy, and just. Proclus says: "Those who desire to reach the highest good have no need for factual knowledge and the exercise of their disposition but only for firmness, quiet, and tranquility of heart. We certainly ought not seek out the highest good or aspire thereto through factual knowledge or any action of our disposition. Rather, we should offer and commend ourselves to the divine light and, after cutting off our senses, rest in that unknown secret unity of beings."

¶228. We wanted to bring forth these points from the philosophy of the ancients not as if all these statements satisfy us, much less as if we desire to prove our philosophy from theirs. [178]. Rather, for the sake of the soul we wished to show that even those ancient philosophers (many of whom went all the way to Egypt to become educated in the Mosaic writings) required a sort of purging of the soul and an elevation and illumination of the soul in the understanding of sacred matters.

¶229. We have said these things about the interpretation of Scripture indeed with too much detail if you should consider the number of pages, but too superficially with respect to the excellence of this subject and the weakness of our mind. It was our intention to add more, especially some ideas worthy of mention which we must especially observe in the shaping of public discourses which apply legitimately-explained Scripture and instructions gathered therefrom to the edification of others. Time, however, is warning us that, having thanked God humbly, we must pick out a landing place and turn the ship landward.

I have read thoroughly this entire erudite treatise and have detected that it is orthodox in every detail. I decree that it is most worthy of publication. Moreover, I pray and desire for the author an increase of the gifts of God and long life to the advantage of the Church.

Given at Dresden, the 27th of February, 1609.
Master Professor Polycarp Leyser

I repeat the same thing in every detail.

Given at Giessa, 25th of June, 1609.
Master Professor Balthasar Mentzer

[179]

BALTHASAR MENTZER
sends hearty greetings to

THE REVEREND AND RENOWNED GENTLEMAN, THE BLESSED DR. JOHANN GERHARD.

I have heard frequently that many very skilled
   Gentlemen are interpreting Holy Writ.
But to give sure fixed rules of interpretation
And set them in an order fit for the Bible,
To show a level path free of errors which
   One can take to the kingdom of truth
Very few gentlemen have dared to attempt.
O renowned Dr. Gerhard, there remain for you
   Greater praise and glorious honor that
You not begrudge godly scholars but with
Your clearly paternal heart share this very
Trustworthy endeavor with your sons
   who love heavenly truth and are zealous
In reading the Word of God.
May the Ruler of eternity preserve you for us
For a long time and bless you with His gifts.
       Farewell.
       —Given at Giessa 25th of June, 1609.
       Τ. ἀνώτερα χαλλιω.

[180]
Type set by and at the expense of Tobias Steinmann, A. D. 1610
At Jena.

www.ingramcontent.com/pod-product-compliance
Lightning Source LLC
LaVergne TN
LVHW020934090426
835512LV00020B/3352